The Most Interesting People in Religion: 250 Anecdotes

David Bruce

Published by David Bruce, 2023.

While every precaution has been taken in the preparation of this book, the publisher assumes no responsibility for errors or omissions, or for damages resulting from the use of the information contained herein.

THE MOST INTERESTING PEOPLE IN RELIGION: 250 ANECDOTES

First edition. October 23, 2023.

ISBN: 979-8223945543

Written by David Bruce.

Table of Contents

Dedication

Dedicated to Carl Eugene Bruce and Josephine Saturday Bruce

My father, Carl Eugene Bruce, died on 24 October 2013. He used to work for Ohio Power, and at one time, his job was to shut off the electricity of people who had not paid their bills. He sometimes would find a home with an impoverished mother and some children. Instead of shutting off their electricity, he would tell the mother that she needed to pay her bill or soon her electricity would be shut off. He would write on a form that no one was home when he stopped by because if no one was home he did not have to shut off their electricity.

The best good deed that anyone ever did for my father occurred after a storm that knocked down many power lines. He and other linemen worked long hours and got wet and cold. Their feet were freezing because water got into their boots and soaked their socks. Fortunately, a kind woman gave my father and the other linemen dry socks to wear.

My mother, Josephine Saturday Bruce, died on 14 June 2003. She used to work at a store that sold clothing. One day, an impoverished mother with a baby clothed in rags walked into the store and started shoplifting in an interesting way: The mother took the rags off her baby and dressed the infant in new clothing. My mother knew that this mother could not afford to buy the clothing, but she helped the mother dress her baby and then she watched as the mother walked out of the store without paying.

***

The doing of good deeds is important. As a free person, you can choose to live your life as a good person or as a bad person. To be a good person, do good deeds. To be a bad person, do bad deeds. If you do good deeds, you will become good. If you do bad deeds, you will become bad. To become the person you want to be, act as if you already are that kind of person. Each of us chooses what kind of person we will become. To become a good person, do the things a good person does. To become a bad person, do the things a bad person does. The opportunity to take action to become the kind of person you want to be is yours.

Human beings have free will. According to the Babylonian Niddah 16b, whenever a baby is to be conceived, the Lailah (angel in charge of contraception) takes the drop of semen that will result in the conception and asks God, "Sovereign of the Universe, what is going to be the fate of this drop? Will it develop into a robust or into a weak person? An intelligent or a stupid person? A wealthy or a poor person?" The Lailah asks all these questions, but it does not ask, "Will it develop into a righteous or a wicked person?" The answer to that question lies in the decisions to be freely made by the human being that is the result of the conception.

A Buddhist monk visiting a class wrote this on the chalkboard: "EVERYONE WANTS TO SAVE THE WORLD, BUT NO ONE WANTS TO HELP MOM DO THE DISHES." The students laughed, but the monk then said, "Statistically, it's highly unlikely that any of you will ever have the opportunity to run into a burning orphanage and rescue an infant. But, in the smallest gesture of kindness — a warm smile, holding the door for the person behind you, shoveling the driveway of the elderly person next door — you have committed an act of immeasurable profundity, because to each of us, our life is our universe."

In her book titled *I Have Chosen to Stay and Fight*, comedian Margaret Cho writes, "I believe that we get complimentary snack-size portions of the afterlife, and we all receive them in a different way." For Ms. Cho, many of her snack-size portions of the afterlife come in hip hop music. Other people get different snack-size portions of the afterlife, and we all must be on the lookout for them when they come our way. And perhaps doing good deeds and experiencing good deeds are snack-size portions of the afterlife.

Photograph for Front Cover of *The Most Interesting People in Religion*:
    https://pixabay.com/illustrations/symbols-religions-faith-835892/

***

This is a short, quick, and easy read.
    Anecdotes are usually short humorous stories. Sometimes they are thought-provoking or informative, not amusing.

***

Educate Yourself
    Read Like A Wolf Eats
    Be Excellent to Each Other
    Books Then, Books Now, Books Forever

***

Do you know a language other than English? If you do, I give you permission to translate this book, copyright your translation, publish or self-publish it, and keep all the royalties for yourself. (Do give me credit, of course, for the original book.)

Chapter 1: From Animals to Clothing

Animals

• When Muhammad, prophet of Islam, left Mecca in the emigration, assassins tried to find him. According to a sacred story of Islam, Muhammad hid in a cave, and overnight an acacia tree grew up in the mouth of the cave. In addition, a spider made a web over the cave's mouth, and a dove built a nest on a rock where a person would have to go to reach the cave. The assassins discovered the cave, but felt it was impossible for anyone to be inside, so they did not enter the cave. (When Muhammad left the cave, he was careful not to disturb the nesting dove.)[1]

• Buddhists believe in reincarnation, meaning that we have all lived many, many lives, including perhaps lives as animals. Buddhist stories include tales of the previous lives of the Buddha; these are known as the Jataka tales. Buddhists strive to be compassionate, and when the Buddha lived a previous life as a rabbit, he vowed to be so compassionate that if a beggar were starving, he would offer his own flesh to save the beggar.[2]

• A man was afraid of dogs. His friends advised him that he would have nothing to fear if he simply recited sacred scripture whenever he saw a dangerous dog. However, the man replied, "I think that I will take a big stick with me just in case the dog doesn't understand sacred scripture."[3]

Authors

• Early in his career — in fact, during his first-ever job as a writer — *Tucson Weekly* columnist Tom Danehy wrote this sentence: "I'd like to see a high school football season go by without a cheerleader getting pregnant." Of course, this is a sentiment that all can agree with, although some people do not care to see it in print. One Cf those people was the publisher, and Tom's career at a writer — at least in that town — seemed likely to end soon, as in immediately. However, the father of a cheerleader, who also happened to be the bishop of the local ward of the Church of Jesus Christ of Latter-day Saints, a big shot in that town, and a close friend of the publisher, saved Tom's job by coming to his defense, even though he and Tom had had some major disagreements. Tom ended up leaving the job, and the town, soon anyway, but he always made a point of talking to the bishop each time he returned to the town. Tom says, "We still disagreed about everything (foremost being that his church, at the time, didn't allow blacks to enjoy full membership), but we were cordial, and it [their relationship] was cool [in a good way]." Tom, of course, still continues to have and express opinions, sometimes controversial, including this one: "I'd like to have a member of the Jehovah's Witnesses come to my door, find out that I'm Catholic and say, 'OK, we won't knock on your door any more. See you in heaven some day.'"[4]

Bar Mitzvah

• Being a celebrity means being able to have celebrity guests at your son's bar mitzvah. Songwriter Sammy Cahn was on his way to his son's bar mitzvah when actor Spencer Tracy asked if he could come along. Other celebrities who came along included George Burns and Gracie Allen, Dean Martin, Tony Curtis and Janet Leigh, and Jack Benny and Mary Livingston.[5]

• Jack Soo acted the part of Detective Nick Yemana on the television sitcom *Barney Miller*. Mr. Soo appeared on the television quiz show *Family Feud*, where he was asked the question, "At what age does a boy become a man?" His answer was, "Thirteen." The star of *Barney Miller*, Hal Linden, asks, "And you thought he was Japanese?"[6]

Baseball

• Many baseball players are religious. Jimmy Piersall was noted for using his bat to scratch a cross in the dirt before hitting. New York Yankee catcher Yogi Berra, who was also very religious, noticed Mr. Piersall do this one game. As soon as Mr. Piersall had made the sign of the cross in the dirt with his bat, Mr. Berra used his glove to rub out the cross, then told him, "Why don't you let God just watch the game?"[7]

• Sparky Anderson, manager of the Cincinnati Reds, used to levy a lot of fines on his players for infractions of the rules, then donate the money to charity. Reds player Bernie Carbo once asked Sparky, "My wife keeps asking me why we get so many thank-yous from the Heart Fund. She can't figure out why I'm making so many contributions. What should I tell her?"[8]

Bible

• A pastor once visited a family and asked if they wanted him to read a passage of Scripture from their Bible. The husband and wife agreed, and so they asked their child to bring into the living room that big book that Mommy and Daddy were always reading. A few moments later, the child returned, carrying a J.C. Penney catalog.[9]

• A man claimed to know a lot about the Bible, but in a Bible class it quickly became apparent that he didn't know as much as he had let on he knew. Still, he was unabashed and claimed, "I know all about that, but I've been sworn to secrecy."[10]

Books

• After moving to Brooklyn, Joe Orlando, an artist for *MAD* magazine, was visited by a priest who wanted to bless each room of his home. Therefore, Mr. Orlando took him throughout his new home. When the priest saw Mr. Orlando's big collection of reference works, he asked if any of the works were on the Catholic Index of Prohibited Books (*Librorum Prohibitorum*). None was, so it seemed as if all were going well. However, the priest asked Mr. Orlando what he did for a living, and Mr. Orlando replied that he was an artist for *MAD* magazine. This shocked the priest, who pointed out, "*That's* on the Index!" The priest did not bless Mr. Orlando's home.[11]

• A Rabbi in Poland once wrote a little book, although many other Rabbis wrote big books. Asked why his book was so little, the Rabbi explained that the people he served worked long, hard hours, and they were tired at the end of the day. If he had written a big book, many people would read a page or two, then go to sleep. But since he had written a little book of distilled wisdom, these people were much more likely to actually read all of it.[12]

Charity

• Rabbi Israel of Vishnitz once paid a visit to a rich banker. The Rabbi sat down, but he remained silent for 20 minutes. Because it is not polite to directly ask a Rabbi why he has come, the rich man could do nothing but sit, squirm, and wonder. Finally, the Rabbi stood up and began to walk away. The rich man then could no longer restrain his curiosity and asked, "Why have you come, Rabbi?" The Rabbi replied that he had come to keep a commandment: "The Talmud says that if someone will be benefited by your pointing out an error to him, then you are obligated to point out his error. But if someone will not correct his ways even if you point out his error, then you are obligated to keep silent. I have come here to keep silent." Hearing this, the rich man begged the Rabbi to point out his error, and the Rabbi told him of a widow who could not pay her mortgage and on whom the banker was foreclosing. "That's not my fault," said the banker. "The bank owns the mortgage, not me." "See," said Rabbi Israel. "I knew that you would do nothing." That night, the rich man was unable to sleep. In the morning, he used his own money to pay off the widow's mortgage.[13]

• Some Rabbis were collecting money for their *yeshiva* [school]. They planned to visit a man named Barbuhin to ask for a donation, but when they heard that he ate simple, inexpensive food, they decided that he would probably not give them much money, so they would visit his home last — if at all — to ask for a donation. However, when they visited him, he told them to tell his wife to give them a measure of gold coins. His wife, who like Barbuhin was a good person, did exactly that, giving them a heaping rather than a level measure. The Rabbis were surprised at Barbuhin's generosity, and they explained why they had felt that he would not give them much money. Barbuhin explained, "I have the right to be economical for my personal needs, but not when it comes to fulfilling my Creator's commandments."[14]

• It is important to show respect for other cultures, and we can examine other religions to discover what truth we can learn from them. When Val Halamandaris compiled his book titled *Faces of Caring*, he wrote about 100 caring people who lived throughout history (and some legendary figures). Along with the text, he included a drawing or a photograph of the person he was writing about. However, for Muhammad, the prophet of Allah and the founder of Islam, he did not include a portrait. Why not? According to Islam, images of Muhammad are forbidden. Therefore, instead of a portrait of Muhammad, Mr. Halamandaris used a verse from the Qu'ran. Translated, the verse says, "I seek refuge with the Lord of the Dawn." One of Muhammad's sayings is this: "Every good act is charity. A man's true wealth hereafter is the good that he does in this world for his fellow man."[15]

• Some charities send free gifts to people they hope will donate or will continue to donate money to them. (These are known as "guilt gifts.") However, as you would expect, sometimes these gifts backfire and get the recipients angry at the charity. An actress friend of *Guardian* columnist Michele Hanson received a gift of slippers from a charity she supported. Angry, she sent the slippers back. When she received a letter asking if she had received the slippers, she grew angrier and sent the letter back. Then they sent her a gift of gloves. This didn't help; after all, the actress had been hoping that the money she had given the charity would be spent on helping the needy, not on providing her with slippers and gloves that she didn't want or need.[16]

• A beggar asked Rabbi Shmelke for alms, but the good Rabbi had no money to give, so he gave the beggar a ring. A few minutes after the beggar left, the good Rabbi's wife entered the house, and he told her what he had done. She exclaimed, "That ring was very valuable! It had a real diamond in it! Run and catch up with the beggar!" Rabbi Shmelke ran after the beggar, caught up with him, and told him, "The ring I gave you is very valuable. It has a real diamond in it. When you sell it, make sure that you get a good price."[17]

• Rabbi Aharon Kotler was an Orthodox sage in the 20th century, and he knew that people would watch him to see what he did. One day, as he was entering a synagogue, he gave money to a beggar, and as he later left the synagogue, he gave more money to the same beggar. Asked why he had done this, Rabbi Kotler said that he was afraid that someone might see him pass the beggar without giving money to him and so conclude that the beggar did not deserve to be helped.[18]

Children

• Moses announced to the Jews that God wanted to give them a gift — the Torah — but that he wanted a guarantee that the Jews would keep the Torah and live by its teachings. The Jews decided that a suitable guarantee would be their valuables such as jewelry and precious metals. Moses went up the mountain to talk to God, but when he returned he said that God wanted a better guarantee before he would give the Torah to the Jews. A woman suggested that the Jews' most precious possessions were their children and so the children should be the Jews' guarantee to God — if God gave the Torah to the Jews, they would teach the Torah to their children and so ensure that its wisdom would be passed from generation to generation. The other Jews agreed, and this time when Moses came down from the mountain after talking to God he was carrying two large tablets.[19]

• Many religions have fun-filled festivals. For example, Hinduism has Holi, which takes place in March and which features a lowering of barriers between the sexes, and between the social classes, and among the various castes in India. People celebrating this festival run around throwing colored powder and colored water on each other. When Holi is celebrated, mothers make sure that their children are wearing old clothes because the children and the clothes are sure to be drenched with color. On this day, giggling children smear red powder and green powder and blue powder and yellow powder on other giggling children.[20]

• Sometimes, second graders don't learn the lessons teachers try to teach them. For example, a Sister was teaching her young school children about Jesus and trying to impart to them a lesson about Jesus' forgiving nature. The Sister said, "When people hurt you, act like Jesus. Give them another chance. Forgive them." The Sister then asked, "What if the person who hurts you is really mean and doesn't like you at all? Think: What would Jesus do then?" One of the children answered, "He'd send them straight to Hell."[21]

• Miriam gave birth to seven sons, all of whom were martyred because they declined to worship idols, even when doing so could save their lives. When her final son was about to be executed, she kissed him and told him to give a message to Abraham, "Say to him: Do not be proud because you were willing to sacrifice your only son — I have sacrificed all my seven sons."[22]

• An Italian child once made a donation to Mother Teresa after celebrating his first Communion. He had asked his parents not to buy him a special suit for the occasion, and not to have a party for him. The child gave to Mother Teresa the money that his parents had saved.[23]

Christmas

• On Christmas Eve of 1943, Albert Szajdholc and his family were hiding in a two-story outbuilding by a Catholic church in Andonno, above the Italian Riviera, trying to stay warm and hoping not to be discovered by anti-Semites. Past midnight, a knock sounded on the door. Mr. Szajdholc opened the door and saw a peasant woman, who gave him a piece of cheese and said, "*Buon natale*," which means "Merry Christmas." Throughout the night, other poor peasants arrived, bringing gifts of food and clothing. The next morning, Mr. Szajdholc met a friend, the barber Giacomo Rossi, and told him what had happened. Mr. Rossi explained that in the church on Christmas Eve, Father Borsotto had spoken about the gifts of the Magi to the Christ child and had said, "Just as our savior couldn't find any lodging and was born in a manger, alone and rejected, so are Jews today alone and rejected. We have two Jewish families in our midst this Christmas, and they too are alone, hungry, hunted for no reason except being Jews." Father Borsotto then said that the people in the church could emulate the Magi and bear gifts to the persecuted. The people in the church had listened and brought gifts to Mr. Szajdholc's family and to the other Jewish family in hiding. Some gifts kept coming after Christmas. Eventually, Mr. Szajdholc and his family had to leave Andonno and stay in the mountains. Usebio and Anna Giordano knew that the Jewish family could not survive at night in the mountains, so they left their barn door unlocked at night so that the Szajdholcs could stay there. The Giordanos also left hot soup for them in the barn at night. The mountains were cold even during the day, and the Szajdholcs stayed in an unheated hut where they were afraid to build a fire — the smoke would reveal their presence. One day, they saw an old woman climbing the mountain to them. She was bringing them hot soup. The Szajdholcs survived the Holocaust.[24]

• During World War II, Army nurses usually made a major effort to celebrate Hanukkah and Christmas, even when they were close to a combat zone. An exception sometimes happened with nurses who were POWs — sometimes it was impossible to celebrate Hanukkah and Christmas. In 1942, Army nurses across the globe celebrated Hanukkah and Christmas. In Arzew, Algeria, nurses decorated a fir tree, using as ornaments stars and candy canes that had been cut out of used plasma containers. They also made 400 pounds of fudge, with the assistance of a kind supply officer. And they sewed 700 Christmas stockings, using red serge that French troops had left behind. In the Philippines, POW nurses were still able to celebrate the holidays. They made boats, dolls, jigsaw puzzles, and toy trains for the children in the POW camp. In Australia, Alice Weinstein was the only Jewish nurse in her unit, so she didn't celebrate Hanukkah in the traditional way. She remembers, "When Christmas came around, you always went through your things to see what you could give away as a little gift. And the cooks in the outfit didn't have a lot to work with, but they always put themselves out at the holidays."[25]

• Bill Talen, who is also known as Reverend Billy, is strongly against the commercialization of Christmas, and he is strongly against materialism in general. When he first saw Times Square in New York City, he was amazed by the crass commercialism of the place, and so he invented the persona of street preacher Reverend Billy as a way to strike back. He is very willing to perform an exorcism of evil demons from cash registers, and he even has a choir: The Church of Stop Shopping Choir. Together, they sing such songs as "Fill the malls with wealthy people," although most people are more familiar with the words "Deck the halls with boughs of holly." Reverend Billy has performed his activism in Starbucks stores, and as a result he was banned from Starbucks stores in California. In fact, Starbucks head honchos once sent a memo to Starbucks rank-and-file employees that was titled "What Should I Do If Reverend Billy Is In My Store?" In 2007, Reverend Billy starred in the documentary *What Would Jesus Buy?*[26]

• During the first half of the 20th century, Christmas trees often were decorated with lighted candles. During a Christmas Eve gift-giving session at a Texas church, a man playing Santa Claus bent over too near one of the candles, and his coat caught on fire. Immediately, Santa hustled himself out of the church so that he could be away from the eyes of the children as he took off his coat and put out the fire. Still, some of the children were understandably upset, but the preacher, Edwin Porter, told them that Santa had said to "tell all you boys and girls that he has another coat in his pack and that he has to hurry on now or he won't make it around to your houses tonight to fill your stockings."[27]

• In 1965, Rabbi Abraham Joshua Heschel participated with Martin Luther King, Jr., in the Selma-to-Montgomery civil rights march; afterward, at the airport in Montgomery, Alabama, he wanted something to eat. A waitress at the snack-bar counter looked at the good Rabbi, with his white hair and beard, and said, "Well, I'll be d*mned. My mother always told me there was a Santa Claus, and I didn't believe her, until now." She also denied that the snack bar had any food. The good Rabbi responded gently, asking if she had water. She did. He also asked if she had eggs. She did. He then requested that she boil some eggs for him — after all, he had done her a favor. "What favor have you ever done me?" she asked. The good Rabbi replied, "I proved there was a Santa Claus." She laughed, and she served food to him.[28]

• During Christmas of 1864, Union General William Tecumseh Sherman was busy making his famous "march to the sea," engaging in destruction of the South as he went. However, despite the devastation he and his troops caused, he did give permission to some Union soldiers to celebrate Christmas. The soldiers made dolls out of rags as well as other crude toys, and they gathered together some of their food to give away to Southerners. They then decorated a wagon to make it look like a sleigh, and they even improvised antlers for the heads of the mules that pulled the wagon. Finally, with a sergeant dressed up as Santa Claus, they delivered the toys and food to homes in Savannah, Georgia.[29]

• Isaac Sztrymfman hid in rural France with a woman named Madame Duvolder, who called him Jean Duvolder. This fooled the Nazis who would have killed Isaac because he was Jewish. Madame Duvolder was a Catholic for whom Christmas was very important. In 1943, Madame Duvolder and Isaac did not have much money to celebrate Christmas with, but they cut down a small evergreen tree and decorated it. On Christmas Eve, Madame Duvolder told Isaac to shine his shoes and leave them under the tree. In the morning, he found his gifts: a scarf that Madame Duvolder had knitted for him, and an orange — a precious gift because of their rarity in wartime France.[30]

• Like many physicians, Thomas S. Cullen occasionally had patients who could not afford urgently needed medical care. One impoverished woman was very worried about the cost of her necessary operation, so he tried to set her at ease by telling her, "I think I know what you want me to do — as much as necessary, but as little as possible." As it turned out, what she and her husband were able to give Dr. Cullen was much appreciated, although its monetary value did not cover the cost of the operation — the woman's very grateful husband left the good doctor a bag of hickory nuts at his door on Christmas Eve.[31]

• Anna Pavlova made Christmas memorable for members of her dance company, many of them teenaged girls. In Montreal, Canada, she arranged a sleigh ride for everybody. Arriving at her hotel, everyone had a feast, then were given the presents, which were hung on a Christmas tree. On another Christmas, the company was on board a shop en route to South Africa. However, in the dining room Ms. Pavlova had placed a Christmas tree, which was loaded with presents. None of her dancers knew how the Christmas tree had gotten on board the ship.[32]

• Three boys — one Catholic, one Protestant, and one Jewish — talked about the holidays. The Catholic boy said, "Christmas is a wonderful day at my house. We go to early Mass, and then we come home and open presents." The Protestant boy said, "Christmas is a wonderful day at my house. We go to church services, and then we come home and open presents." The Jewish boy said, "Christmas is a wonderful day at my house. We go to my father's store, look at all the empty shelves, and then we go home and sing, 'What a Friend We Have in Jesus.'"[33]

• Cultures differ from country to country. In 1909, Italian baritone Enrico Pignataro arrived in New York just before Christmas. He was shocked to see many wreaths hanging on front doors because in his country a wreath on the door meant that someone in that house had recently died. Mr. Pignataro wrote back home: "I have arrived safely, but a plague has hit this city. People are dying like flies. There are wreaths on almost every door. Light many candles for me, and pray that I may leave this place alive."[34]

• Children's book author Jean Marzollo once decided to research how Native Americans celebrate Christmas. One woman told her the story of her son, John Beane, who had been weak as an infant. His family gave him the gift of an eagle feather because an eagle is strong. John became strong like the eagle, and his family celebrated Christmas each year by placing that eagle feather at the top of their Christmas tree. Ms. Marzollo used that story in her book *The Best Present Ever*.[35]

• Elite gymnasts have to watch what they eat. Very often, their low-fat meals consist of chicken, rice, salad, and for a treat, fruit. At a 1991 Christmas party at world-class women's gymnastics coach Bela Karolyi's ranch, the elite gymnasts gave a skit in which one gymnast made fun of their diet by pretending to be Bela's wife, Marta, telling the gymnasts, "And for dinner, since it's Christmas, you get *two* grapes!"[36]

• Maureen Lipman, as a junior member of an acting company, once performed in Neil Simon's *Chapter Two* with the great actor Sir Laurence Olivier. For Christmas, she gave him a book. He wrote her a thank-you letter, beginning with an apology for not writing sooner. At the end of the letter — four handwritten pages — he apologized for being so brief.[37]

• At one hectic Christmas in the house of Quaker humorist Tom Mullen, a mother tried to calm the children by saying, "Remember, all these gifts come from Jesus." Another adult responded, "Then let's send the bill to him."[38]

• Christmas can be a hectic time. If we let commercialism take over, all the joy can be taken out of Christmas. Once, a small girl prayed, "Forgive us our Christmases as we forgive those who Christmas against us."[39]

Church

• In the 19th century, many clergymen regarded going to theaters as sinful. The great 19th-century actor Joseph Jefferson once received a letter from a clergyman who asked him to perform *Rip Van Winkle* in his church, as he never went to the theater. Mr. Jefferson wrote back to say that honoring his request was impossible because he never went to church.[40]

• When "Shoeless Joe" Jackson was attending Brandon Baptist Church after retiring from baseball, the pastor of the church, the Reverend Boyd Turner, used to stand in front of Shoeless Joe's liquor store each Friday as a signal for him to open the till, take out his tithe, and give it to the pastor for the use of the church.[41]

Clothing

• Catherine Shipley was both a Quaker and the second wife of Murray Shipley, who lived in Cincinnati, Ohio. She was conservative in her dress and didn't believe in short skirts. While in England, she stayed at a hotel where she was shocked by the short skirts of the young English women she saw. A gentleman and two women from East India walked into the hotel — the women were covered in cloth from head to toe. Ms. Shipley surveyed the women's dress, then told the gentleman, "I congratulate thee on being a heathen." The East India gentleman knew that she was talking about the women's clothing, and he took the compliment well, replying, "Madam, I think the same thing."[42]

• Dodger pitcher Carl Erskine joined the Masons, whose symbol is a big 'G' in the center of a square and compass — God is at the center of Masonic activities. He saw second baseman Jim Gilliam wearing a belt with a buckle decorated with the Masonic symbol. Mr. Erskine told him, "Good-looking belt buckle." He replied, "Yes, I really like it." Thinking of the symbol's religious significance, Mr. Erskine said, "I guess it has a lot of meaning for you." Mr. Gilliam replied, "Oh, yes. I saw this in a store window in Chicago and went right in and bought it. I think it's great. It has my initial right in the middle.[43]

• In Cleveland, Ohio, Father Michael Hayduk was the pastor of St. Mary's Byzantine Catholic Church. While he was visiting the church's day care and pre-school, a 3-year-old boy asked him, "Why do you dress funny?" Father Hayduk explained about his clerical collar and showed the boy his plastic collar insert. On the reverse side of the collar insert was embossed the name of the manufacturer, and Father Hayduk asked the boy, "Do you know what those words say?" The little boy couldn't read, but he replied, "Yes, I do! It says, 'Kills ticks and fleas up to six months.'"[44]

• As a young student at Notre Dame Convent, young Patricia Wilde was scheduled to dance in a short-skirted elf costume. (Short skirts are common in dance to show off the legs, which of course are an important part of dance.) However, when the nuns saw her costume, they immediately began to pin streamers to the skirt to make the hemline longer. Young Patricia protested that the nuns were *ruining* her costume — to no avail. (Since then, she has danced many, many times in a tutu — the shortest imaginable skirt.)[45]

Chapter 2: From Death to Food

Death

• Folk tales can contain truth, even if it is not literal truth. Death, who brings death to all living things, was near death one day, but a happy young man saw him and took care of him, saving him. In gratitude, Death said that he would not arrive suddenly on the day that the man was to die, but that he would first send messengers to remind the man that he would die one day. The man lived long and mostly happily, but at times he grew ill and occasionally he even wished that he were dead. One day Death arrived and told the man that it was his day to die. The man was shocked and asked, "Have you forgotten your promise to me? You said that you were going to send messengers to remind me that I would die one day." Death said, "I did send messengers. Every time that you were ill, and especially those times when you wished that you were dead, was a reminder that you would die one day."[46]

• This is good advice: Repent one day before you die. Of course, few of us are aware much in advance of the day that we will die. (Even condemned prisoners often have the date of their execution changed.) Therefore, we should repent our sins each and every day and avoid sin each and every day. Rabbi Yochanan ben Zakkai told a parable about a King who told his people to be prepared for when he would hold a banquet. Some of the people thought that the banquet would be held far in the future, so they did not bother to get ready for the banquet since they would have time to do so later. Other, wiser people immediately began preparing for the banquet, realizing that although the banquet could be held far in the future, it could also be held immediately. As it happened, the banquet was held quickly, and only the people who were ready were admitted to the banquet hall.[47]

• Not everyone who dies of AIDS is a gay man or an illegal drug user. Daisy was born with AIDS; her father was a bisexual who infected

15

Daisy's mother, who then passed the disease on to Daisy. Daisy's mother, an Englishwoman, took care of her, and Daisy was most comfortable when her mother held her, which meant that her mother got very little sleep. One thing that little Daisy did that made her mother happy was to make a kiss-kiss motion with her mouth, which made her mother feel like Daisy was telling her, "It's all right, Mummy." Before Daisy died, she was paralyzed and her body was very twisted, but her mother says that as the life and pain left her body, "She became perfectly straight, and she looked beautiful. Her blonde hair was like a halo, going round her face."[48]

• In April of 1993 at Washington D.C., Holocaust survivor Elie Wiesel spoke at the dedication of the Holocaust Memorial Museum. He told the story of a woman in the Carpathian Mountains 50 years previously who had heard about the rebellion of the Jews in Warsaw, Poland, and who could not understand why they were fighting. She asked, "Why are our Jews in Warsaw behaving like this? Why are they fighting? Couldn't they have waited patiently until the end of the war?" This woman was unaware of the concentration camps and of why the Jews were fighting. One year passed, and then she and her family were forced onto cattle cars and taken to Auschwitz. Mr. Wiesel then told the crowd, "She was my mother." She did not survive the Holocaust.[49]

• One night, the Sisters of the Missionaries of Charity went around the streets of Calcutta and picked five or six abandoned people, then brought them to the Home for the Dying and the Abandoned. Mother Teresa was preparing to put a little old lady to bed, but the little old lady told her, "Thank you," then died. Mother Teresa asked herself what she would have done if she were in the little old lady's position: "And I answered with honesty. Surely I would have done all I could to draw attention to myself. I would have shouted, 'I'm hungry! I'm dying of thirst! I'm dying!' She, on the other hand, was so grateful, so unselfish.

She was so generous! The poor — I do not tire of repeating this — are wonderful."[50]

• At Auschwitz, Dr. Josef Mengele performed horrible experiments on pregnant women that left both the women and their fetuses dead. Therefore, Dr. Gisella Perl, who was in Auschwitz, became determined that no more women would be pregnant in Auschwitz. She performed abortions whenever they were needed, feeling bad because she was killing a fetus, but knowing that the abortion was necessary to keep Dr. Mengele from killing both the fetus and its mother. After the Holocaust ended, she worked delivering babies, and she always prayed to God before delivering a baby, "God, you owe me a life: a living baby."[51]

• In 1974, Muhammad Ali fought in Zaire for the championship title. Before leaving, he visited a child who had leukemia. Mr. Ali told the child, "I am going to Africa and win back my title. I'm going to win my battle. And you're going to win yours." Mr. Ali won his battle, but the child was dying. Mr. Ali again visited the child and said, "I told you that we were going to win our battles together. I won mine; now you are going to win yours." The child looked at Mr. Ali and replied, "No, I'm going to heaven to meet God, and I'm going to tell Him that I knew you, and that you were my friend."[52]

• A woman mourned the death of her child, and she went from door to door hoping to find someone who could bring the child back to life. Arriving at a Buddhist temple, she met a priest who responded to her that he could bring her child to life if she would find a family that had never known death, borrow five poppy seeds from them, and bring the poppy seeds to the priest. The woman searched for a family that had never known death, but she quickly discovered that every family had known death. Realizing that death is inevitable, she buried her child.[53]

• When the father of James J. Reyor died, a mix-up in communication occurred between the hospital and the funeral home, so his father's body was late for his own wake. An empty, closed coffin had to be displayed at the funeral home because the body was still at the hospital. One man couldn't understand why the casket was closed, so Mr. Reyor explained that it was empty. The man asked, "Where's your father?" Mr. Reyor replied, "He's still at the hospital." Surprised, the man then asked, "Aren't you rushing things a bit?"[54]

• Some people live their lives according to how they perceive God wants them to live their lives. When the ancient teacher Confucius was dying, his disciples asked if they should pray for him. Confucius replied, "My life has been my prayer." Earlier, he had been appointed to the post of minister of justice for the duke of Lu. However, the duke of Lu was given 80 women. Confucius advised him to turn down the decadent gift. The duke of Lu refused, and Confucius resigned his highly coveted position.[55]

• Isolde, Oscar Wilde's sister, died in 1867 at the age of 10. Oscar, aged 13, decorated an envelope and put a lock of his sister's hair in it — it was one of his few remaining possessions at his death. The decorations included his initial and her initial joined together, and this quotation from Mark, ch. 5, verse 39: "She is not dead but sleepeth." He also wrote his poem "Requiescat" about his sister.[56]

• Even on the day that Thomas More died, he was able to make jokes. On 16 July 1535, he dressed in his best clothing, knowing that he was to be beheaded that day. Climbing up the scaffold, he told the executioner, "I pray thee see me safe up, and for my coming down, let me shift for myself!" Before he was beheaded, he asked that his beard be spared — after all, *it* was not accused of treason.[57]

• When Hazel von Jeschki died at the age of 94, she left very specific directions for choosing her pallbearers. She wrote, "There will be no male pallbearers. They wouldn't take me out when I was alive; I don't want them to take me out when I'm dead."[58]

• This epitaph appears on a Scottish gravestone: "Dry up your tears and weep no more, / I am not dead but gone before, / Remember me and bear in mind, / You have not long to stay behind."[59]

Easter

• Sean Gonsalves, a reporter for the *Cape Cod Times*, tells this story: At the University of Chicago Divinity School there used to be held "Baptist Day," on which the entire surrounding Baptist community was invited to come to the school, hear a lecture, mingle, and eat a bag lunch. One Baptist Day, the speaker was Protestant theologian Paul Tillich. Mr. Tillich spoke about the resurrection of Jesus, arguing that the resurrection was not to be understood literally. As he argued, Mr. Tillich demonstrated his great learning. After Mr. Tillich had finished his lecture, he asked if there were any questions. An aged African-American Baptist preacher stood up and spoke, and as he spoke he peeled and ate an apple. He said, "I ain't never read them books you read." Here he paused to take a bite of the apple, then added, "and I can't recite the Scriptures in the original Greek." Again, he ate some of the apple, then said, "I don't know nothing about Niebuhr and Heidegger, but all I want to know is: This apple I just ate — was it bitter or sweet?" Mr. Tillich replied, "I cannot possibly answer that question, for I haven't tasted your apple." The Baptist preacher said, "Neither have you tasted my Jesus."[60]

• A man who wanted to start a new religion approached Voltaire for advice. Voltaire told him, "I would advise that you first get yourself crucified, then rise on the third day."[61]

Education

• After five years as a Redemptorist, Father John Neumann was appointed vicegerent of the order's American branch. As such, he did much traveling, and one day he visited the Redemptorist house in New York. Met by the porter, he asked to see the pastor of the house. The porter started off to get the pastor, and Father Neumann began to follow him, but the porter told him, "Stay here, if you please. Take a seat on that bench, while I call the superior." Then the porter muttered his thoughts loud enough for Father Neumann to hear him, "This man thinks he can enter the cloister." Quickly, the porter reappeared and asked Father Neumann for his name. Hearing the answer, the porter told him, "Oh, if you are one of the priests, do come in." The porter was then astonished to see the superior of the house kneel and ask Father Neumann for his blessing, and the porter left quickly. Later, Father Neumann had a meeting with the porter and told him that yes, he had fulfilled faithfully his duty as a porter. However, Father Neumann added gently, "I think it might be wise not to think out loud."[62]

• Musician Naomi Judd hosted a cable-TV talk show on Sunday mornings, and if she could have any guest she wanted, she would have Jesus as her guest. During a break while appearing on Larry King's talk show, she asked him whom he would like to have as a guest. Mr. King replied, "God." She then asked him what would be his first question. Mr. King replied, "I would ask Him if He had a Son." Ms. Judd has long taken religion seriously. Her mother tells a story about when Naomi was a child. Her mother met Naomi's Sunday-School teacher, who told her that she had to be extra prepared to teach her Sunday-School lessons because Naomi was sure to ask questions such as "Would you explain that Immaculate Conception just one more time?" and "OK, how did He raise Lazarus from the dead?" As a young adult, she almost gave her mother a stroke when she told her mother that she had visited a Buddhist temple — as it happened, just to check it out. She also worked an extra shift as a young adult so she could buy the Time-Life series of books on the Great Religions.[63]

• Authors and illustrators often acquire special knowledge. For example, Paul Goble, who retells Native American folk tales in his books for children, has learned, "I cannot be creative when using a machine." Therefore, he writes his stories in longhand, then uses an old typewriter to type what he has just created. (Of course, other people are able to be creative when using machines such as personal computers.)

He does like old things, such as the recorders that his father, a maker of harpsichords, made in the 1930s and 1940s. Paul and Robert, his son, played duets on these recorders. Another thing Paul has learned is that it is sometimes better to draw something rather than to take a photograph of it because drawing requires the artist to look closely. Yet another thing he has learned is that the spirits will help you if you are persistent. A Native American woman once wrote him, "I've always thought the *wanga* (spirits) are close to you. Some of your illustrations reveal that the ancestors come to visit you in your dreams."[64]

• Rabbi Levi Yitzchak of Berdichev arrived at a town where he asked a rich man for hospitality; however, the rich man, not knowing that his visitor was distinguished, told him to ask an impoverished teacher for hospitality. The Rabbi did so, and the teacher welcomed him. The next day, word spread through the town that the distinguished Rabbi Levi Yitzchak was visiting. The rich man immediately invited the Rabbi to stay at his house, pointing out that it was much more luxurious than the house of the teacher. However, the Rabbi declined, saying that two kinds of hospitality existed. One was the hospitality of Abraham, who, when angels came to him, thought the angels were Arabs, yet gave them hospitality. The other was the hospitality of Lot, who gave hospitality to the angels only after being sure that they were in fact angels. Your hospitality, Rabbi Yitzchak said to the rich man, is unfortunately the hospitality of Lot.[65]

• A man once went to his Rabbi and confessed, "I have slandered my friend by lying about him and speaking evilly about him. What is to be my punishment?" The Rabbi answered, "Go to the town square with a feather pillow. Cut open the feather pillow and let the feathers fly into the wind. Then come back to see me." The man did as he was told, then returned to the Rabbi and asked, "I have cut open the feather pillow and let the feathers fly into the wind. But how is that supposed to punish me?" The Rabbi answered, "That is only the first — the easy — part of your punishment. Now you must go and collect all the feathers you let fly into the wind. Releasing feathers — and words — into the wind is easy; gathering them again is difficult."[66]

• Confucianism is highly concerned with ethics and ethical conduct. When Confucius was the chief magistrate of the town of Zhongdu, he taught the people ethics. One day, a man lost his wallet in the streets. The wallet remained on the streets for a few days because no one would pick it up because it did not belong to him or her; eventually, the man who had lost the wallet returned to the street, saw his wallet, and picked it up. Centuries after the death of Confucius, his teachings, including his belief that a widow ought not to remarry, were still influential in China. When a Chinese emperor learned that in Vietnam, a widow was free to remarry, he was so shocked that he sent to Vietnam 10,000 copies of a book by Confucius about how women ought to behave.[67]

• Brazilian novelist Paulo Coelho once undertook a course of study called the "feminine way" or the "Road to Rome" in which he hoped to discover his feminine side and learn compassion. Like some kinds of psychoanalysis, the course of study involved paying attention to dreams. In addition, the person would have to go to the location of the dream and see what happened. When Mr. Coelho told his master that he couldn't remember his dreams, his master told him that everyone has dreams. Mr. Coelho then said, "Well, I dreamt of a garage." His master replied, "What do you want to dream of, the Virgin Mary? Go find a garage and see what happens."[68]

• One of the things that Taibai learned from Zen master Baso was that mind is Buddha. After Taibai had himself been a Zen master for several years, Baso decided to test him. He sent a monk to him to ask, "What did you learn from Master Baso?" Taibai replied that he had learned that mind is Buddha. The monk, as instructed, then said, "Master Baso has now changed his way of teaching. He now teaches that mind is not Buddha." Taibai then replied, "When will that old man stop trying to confuse people? Let him teach what he wants. For me, mind is Buddha." The monk reported to Baso what Taibai had said, and Baso was very pleased.[69]

• Zen master Bankei was preparing to leave a certain spot, when a messenger of a nobleman arrived, asking him to remain for another day, so that the nobleman could confer with him about a certain matter. Bankei agreed to stay, but at the time appointed for the conference with the nobleman, a messenger arrived, saying that the nobleman had been detained but had said that the messenger could convey Bankei's advice to him. Bankei declined to do this, saying, "This matter of Zen is difficult to convey even by direct question and direct answer; it is all the more difficult to convey by messenger."[70]

• Astronomer Cecilia Payne-Gaposchkin was born in England, where she attended a religious school when she was a child, but she was very interested in science and decided to take the entrance exams for Cambridge University. Part of the exams required translating religious passages from Latin and Greek. Her religious training came in handy here. She was able to recognize the religious passages and rather than translate them, she simply wrote them from memory. Later, she became Harvard University's first woman full professor and first woman head of a department.[71]

• A young man became the disciple of a spiritual master and was assigned the task of cleaning the latrines in the monastery. The young man's mother, who was a physician, was displeased at her son's being assigned this task and so she sent the spiritual master several servants, asking that they be the ones assigned to clean the latrines. The spiritual master sent the servants back to the wealthy woman, along with this message: "You are a physician. If your son suffered from a physical disease, should I give the medicine to a servant instead of giving it to him?"[72]

• A samurai once commanded a monk, "Teach me about heaven and hell." The monk replied, "I can't teach you anything because you're too stupid to learn. You know absolutely nothing, including how to be a samurai. Go away. I can't stand you." The samurai became furious and drew his sword to kill the monk. "That's hell," said the monk. The samurai then was filled with compassion and gratitude because the monk had shown him what hell was. "And that's heaven," said the monk.[73]

• A Sister, the principal of a Catholic elementary school, faced a problem when she received a note from a teacher saying that a young boy had gone to the bathroom and had not returned to class. The Sister went into the bathroom for young boys and found the truant in a stall. She asked if the boy was OK, and the boy said that he was. She then asked if the boy was ready to go back to the classroom, and the boy asked, "Is phonics almost over?"[74]

• R' Yosef's father died, and many great Torah scholars came to comfort him. The Torah scholars became involved in a discussion of the Torah, and R' Yosef joined in the discussion. Afterward, he was asked whether it was true that Torah study was forbidden for the first seven days of mourning. R' Yosef replied, "I know that I committed a sin, and that I will surely be punished for it. But it is worthwhile being punished for the study of the Torah."[75]

• Some parents have different priorities for their children than other parents. Elementary schoolteacher Penelope H. Bevan once had a conference with a parent who was a follower of the Sikh religion. The man's daughter was brilliant, and Ms. Bevan showed him some samples of her work, but he was interested in something else. He told Ms. Bevan, "Yes, yes, I know she is quite smart, but I want to know how her soul is developing."[76]

• King Wej was depressed and unable to enjoy life, so he said to Si-tien, a Buddhist priest, "I am troubled, I am pained, and nothing gives me pleasure. What shall I do?" Si-tien took King Wej to see King Hsu, who sat on his mat, talking, smiling, laughing, eating, and drinking with other people. Si-tien then told King Wej, "Sit down near him, and do as he does. Joy is something to be learned."[77]

• Sun-tu once asked the Buddhist priest Si-tien why Lu, an old peasant, was continually harassed by men much more powerful than himself: "Why is this happening? Obviously this old peasant Lu has nothing." Si-tien replied, "Yes, he has." Sun-tu asked, "What can he possibly have that very powerful men can lack?" Si-tien replied, "Dignity."[78]

• A pupil named Lin-sien once asked the Buddhist priest Si-tien, "Should one live life with the expectation of being safe or with awareness that danger may strike?" To answer this question, Si-tien grabbed a small object nearby and put it in Lin-sien's hands. The object was a snake, which bit Lin-sien. Si-tien then said, "Life should be lived with the awareness that danger may strike."[79]

• Lessons can be learned in strange ways. John Wesley and Samuel Bradburn once witnessed an angry quarrel between two women who used bad language but who used it passionately and well and with their whole being. Mr. Bradburn was disgusted by the language and wanted to leave, but Mr. Wesley told him, "Stay — and learn how to preach."[80]

• When she was a child, astronomer Cecilia Payne-Gaposchkin attended a religious school where religion was emphasized over science. Nevertheless, young Cecilia prepared herself to go on to study science when she was older. When she won a prize at the religious school, she requested that she be given a book on fungi.[81]

• Trevor Huddleston, an Anglican priest, worked tirelessly against apartheid in South Africa. One of the things he did was to operate a school for South African children. In his opinion, the best compliment he received in his life came from an African student, who said about him, "I wish he was black."[82]

• Rabbi Yoizel believed in keeping in contact with and exhorting his pupils. When letters became dangerous to send because of war, he sent his pupils short telegrams bearing such messages as "IF NOT

NOW, WHEN THEN?" and "DO PENANCE!" and "IF NOT YOU, WHO WILL?"[83]

• The originator of Hassidism — the Baal Shem Tov, or the Besht — was a teacher of children. As a teacher's assistant (a *behelfer*) he was popular. Instead of whipping the small children he taught, as so many other teachers of the time did, he led them to school, singing as they went.[84]

• R. Uri used to study scripture until late at night, and then rise late in the morning. Once he was asked why he didn't go to bed early and then rise early the next morning to study sacred scripture. He replied, "How do I know that I will rise the next morning?"[85]

Evil

• How evil were the people of Sodom? When a stranger arrived in their city, each citizen would give him a piece of gold that had been marked with the name of the giver. The stranger would be grateful, of course, to receive the gold, but he would quickly find that he was unable to spend it. Each time he would attempt to buy food, the shop owners would refuse to sell it to him. In addition, the stranger found that he was unable to leave the city — the guards would not allow him to pass the gates. Therefore, the stranger — despite his pile of gold coins — would slowly starve to death. When the stranger had starved to death, the citizens would come by the pile of gold coins, pick up the coin with their name marked on it and wait to starve to death another stranger.[86]

• The Emperor Adrianus asked Rabbi Joshua why God's name is mentioned only in the first five of the 10 Commandments, but not in the last five, which include "Do not murder," "Do not commit adultery," and "Do not steal," in the words of the Good News Bible. Rabbi Joshua walked over the town with the Emperor and showed him his statue in many public places, then he showed the Emperor some bathrooms, where his statues were not on display. Then he said that just as the Emperor's statues were not to be found in dirty places, so

God's name is not to be associated with such evils as murder, sexual immorality, and theft.[87]

• One teaching of the Buddhist priest Si-tien was this: "You cannot push away the evil; you can only destroy it." One day, Li-tie visited Si-tien, leaving his sandals outside, and asked him to explain what this teaching meant. Si-tien replied, "There is a piece of dog dung on the threshold. Please clean it up." Li-tie got a stick and flipped the piece of dung outside Si-tien's hut. Si-tien then said, "Bring me some fresh water from the spring." Li-tie went outside for a moment, then he returned and told Si-tien, "The path to the spring is rocky, and when I flipped the dog dung outside I flipped it on my sandals." Si-tien replied, "Not only evil creates evil. It can be created by each careless act."[88]

• Hinduism has an exorcism ceremony that is performed when something very bad happens. In 2001, a mass murder was committed at the palace of the king of Nepal, whose son gunned down the entire family, then committed suicide. Therefore, Hindus performed the *katto* ceremony to purify the community and to banish evil influences. A senior Brahmin priest rode an elephant while people chased him out of the city. The ceremony symbolically showed the late king's spirit carrying away evil from the city.[89]

• A college student was very upset because of the evil that is in the world. He angrily prayed, "The world is filled with problems. I could make a better world than this." God then spoke to the student: "That is exactly what you are supposed to do."[90]

Family

• Mother Teresa once visited a magnificent home for senior citizens in England. Each of its 40 residents was well cared for by the staff; however, none of the 40 residents smiled. Instead, they kept looking at the door of the home. Mother Teresa asked a Sister about this, and the Sister replied, "The same thing always happens. They are always waiting for someone to come to visit them. They dream of a son or a daughter, some member of the family, or a friend coming through that door to visit them." According to Mother Teresa, "The poverty of having no one coming to visit them is the poverty that older people feel the most."[91]

• After boxer George Foreman became a Christian, he started preaching on street corners. One of the people listening to him, although George didn't know it, was his estranged father, J.D. Foreman, who had long been an alcoholic. Hidden, his father listened to him, then told George's mother, "You know, something's happened to that boy. I got to find out what it is." According to George, his father "never took another drink." Instead, George and his father went to church together. George called his father "Brother Foreman," and his father called George "the preacher." Today, George is an ordained minister.[92]

• Comedian Joe E. Brown got married three times to the same woman and never got a divorce. As an impoverished acrobat, he married his wife in an inexpensive civil ceremony, but promised her when they could afford it, they would get married in a fancy church wedding — which they did, 25 years later. A few years after the fancy church wedding, Mrs. Brown said that she wanted to be married by a Catholic priest, since she was Catholic. Mr. Brown agreed to her request, then added, "If it will make you any happier, let a Rabbi marry us, too."[93]

• Mahalia Jackson's first recording session included the gospel song "God Shall Wipe Away All Tears." The song ended up in jukeboxes in her native New Orleans (she was now living in Chicago), and members of her family crowded into a tavern (including some who had never been in a tavern before) to listen to Mahalia sing. Her proud father, Johnny Jackson, listened, then shouted, "That's my daughter!"[94]

Food

• Survivors of the Holocaust often had little or no food to eat. Yvonne Sokolow was a hidden child of the Holocaust, living with various families, many of whom were suffering from food shortages.

Yvonne lived for a while with her mother in a home whose head could provide food for only his family. Yvonne and her mother ate hard bread and soup made from potato peelings, although sometimes they smelled the bacon and eggs that the head of the family could provide only for his family. Yvonne was 17 when World War II ended. She came to the United States, went to Columbia University, got married, and raised a family. She says now, "I will never say about a restaurant, 'I can't eat here,' because it is never as terrible as what I ate during the war." Of course, in her life after the Holocaust her teenage sons would sometimes open the refrigerator at home, look inside, and say that there was nothing to eat. She would always tell them, "You don't know what nothing to eat is like."[95]

• Some people risk much for their religion. For example, at Auschwitz, a man traded 10 pieces of bread — a very valuable commodity — for a pair of tefillin that another person had smuggled into the death camp. Each morning, the prisoners who shared quarters with the man would take turns putting on the tefillin. According to Holocaust survivor Elie Wiesel, "We didn't even have time to say the *Shema*, just the blessing itself. We knew we'd be beaten if we were caught. But we still never missed putting on the tefillin." (Tefillin are small black boxes that contain Jewish sacred writing. During weekday morning prayer, except for holidays, one tefillin is placed on the forehead, and the other is placed on the arm.)[96]

• Welcoming gay people into your church can have its benefits. The Center for Spiritual Living in Seattle welcomes many affinity groups: lesbians, gay men, singles, couples, and elders. The affinity groups contribute to the center in many ways, including taking care of the refreshments served in the Fellowship Hall between services. For example, when it was the gay men's turn to take care of refreshments in autumn, they made a beautiful autumnal centerpiece and served pumpkin spice muffins that had just come out of the oven. Center member Ralph Sanders says, "If this is sin, brother, bring it on!"[97]

• One frontier preacher liked his food spicy and so he carried around a bottle of tabasco sauce. A cowboy once saw him eating some, so he asked if he could try some, too. The cowboy splashed a generous helping on his steak, took a bite, and then drank a large quantity of water. After cooling his throat, the cowboy asked, "Parson, you do preach hellfire, don't you?" The answer came back, "Indeed, I do." The cowboy then said, "You're the first preacher I ever saw who carried a sample around in his pocket." From then on, the preacher was called "Hellfire."[98]

• Saint Teresa of Avila knew that for everything there is a season. Once, a visitor came to see her and was astonished to see her dining on roast partridge that had been given to her — after all, are holy people supposed to do that? She simply said, "There is a time for penance, and there is a time for partridge. Now is the time for partridge!" Not surprisingly, Teresa of Avila once prayed, "Lord, deliver me from sour-faced saints!"[99]

• After many years in America, a Jew went back to Europe to visit his old hometown and find out news about his old friends. He visited a Hasidic Rabbi, who was eating, and asked about many old friends. But no matter whom he asked about, the Rabbi replied, "He's dead" or "She's dead." Shocked, the American Jew asked, "Are all of my old friends dead?" The Rabbi replied, "Only while I'm eating."[100]

• Two feisty Church of Christ preachers, A.G. Freed and Foy E. Wallace, Jr., were invited to dinner. Their hostess asked them if they wanted coffee. Mr. Freed was against drinking coffee, so he said, "No, I'm a Christian." Mr. Wallace saw that this remark embarrassed the hostess, so he said, "Pour me a cup. I'm a Christian, too, but I didn't let it make a fool out of me."[101]

• Once a teacher asked a little boy, "Did you say your prayers before eating?" "No," the boy replied. "It's not necessary — my mom is a good cook."[102]

Chapter 3: From God to Marriage

God

• God exists, and yet people are skeptical about the existence of God. God created everything, and therefore, God created skepticism about His existence. Why would God do that? According to Rabbi Moses Loeb, God created skepticism about His existence in order to help the poor. Because of skepticism about the existence of God, rich people cannot tell poor people, "God will take care of you," and rich people cannot tell poor people, "Your reward will be in the world to come." Because of skepticism about the existence of God, rich people are obligated to help poor people right now, in this world.[103]

• Rabbi Shneur Zalman, the Rabbi of Northern White Russia, was placed in prison by the opponents of Hasidism. While he was awaiting trial, a jailor asked him why God, who is omniscient, walked in the Garden of Eden after Adam had hid himself, and asked, "Where art thou?" The Rabbi first explained that the Scriptures are true and that they apply to every person, then he replied, "In every era, God calls to every man, 'Where are you in your world? So many years and days of those allotted to you have passed, and how far have you gotten in your world?'"[104]

• A man once complained to Menachem Mendel of Kotzk, "God created the world in six days — and look, it's ugly!" The good Rabbi asked the man if he could do a better job than God. The man replied that yes, he could. The good Rabbi then said, "What are you waiting for? Start working — right now!"[105]

• George Whitefield (1714-1770) and John Wesley (1703-1791) differed on a few points of theological interpretation. Knowing this, someone asked Mr. Whitefield if he expected to see Mr. Wesley in Heaven. "No, sir, I fear not," Mr. Whitefield replied, "for he will be so near the throne and we shall be at such a distance, we shall hardly get sight of him."[106]

• The Rabbi of Kotzk once asked, "Where is the dwelling of God?" The learned scholars to whom he asked this question laughed at him, for they felt that the World was filled with His glory, so the Rabbi of Kotzk answered his own question: "God dwells wherever man lets him in."[107]

• Amy Lowell intensely disliked the members of the Cabot family. Once, she was about to sail to Europe, but she suddenly disembarked, saying, "There are 16 Cabots aboard that ship and God is unlikely to forego such a wonderful opportunity."[108]

Good Deeds

• A poor family that was traveling by wagon got stuck in the mud and needed help. A rich man who rode in a fancy carriage came across them. This rich man was not known for charity; in fact, whenever a poor person came to his door to beg for charity, the rich man's servant — following a standing order from the rich man — turned away the poor person. However, it is quite different to actually see someone who needs help and not do something to help them. Therefore, the rich man helped this poor family to get their wagon out of the mud, although he got quite muddy helping them, and he gave them money to help them continue on their journey. When the rich man died, he went to the place of judgment, where his good deeds were put on one side of the scales and his bad deeds were put on the other side of the scales. The rich man's bad deeds weighed more than his good deeds, and it looked as if the rich man would be condemned to Hell. However, Saint Peter asked if any good deed had been overlooked. An angel replied, "As you know, an angel is created whenever a human being does a good deed. I was created when this rich man helped a poor family get its wagon unstuck from the mud." Saint Peter said, "Put the poor family on the scales, and let's see if that will tip the scales toward Paradise." The angel swept up a very surprised poor family and put them on the scales, but the scales still tipped toward Hell, not Paradise. "Wait a moment," the angel said, "I have an idea." The angel disappeared, and then returned with the mud that had stuck to the rich man when he had helped the poor family get its wagon unstuck from the mud. The angel placed the mud on the scales, and they tipped toward Paradise.[109]

• During the Holocaust, Oskar Schindler saved the lives of more than 1,200 Jews. His good deed is known today largely because of one of the Jews he saved: Poldek Pfefferberg, who lived in the United States under the name of Leopold Page. He told Mr. Schindler, "You protect us, you save us, you feed us — we survived the Holocaust, the tragedy, the hardship, the sickness, the beatings, the killings! We must tell your story!" In Beverly Hills, Mr. Page operated a store for the sale and repair of leather goods. His customers were authors, actors, directors, and producers. Whenever anyone came in, Mr. Page told them the story of Oskar Schindler and tried to get them interested in writing or telling Mr. Schindler's story. In 1980, Australian author Thomas Keneally came into the store to buy a briefcase, heard the story, and wrote the book *Schindler's List* with Mr. Page as an advisor. In 1982, after much research, including interviews with 50 Jews in seven countries whom Mr. Schindler had saved, Mr. Keneally's book — a classic — appeared. Later, Stephen Spielberg made a movie of Mr. Keneally's book, and again Mr. Page was an advisor. It took Mr. Spielberg 11 years to start making the movie, and once a week for 11 years Mr. Page called Mr. Spielberg's office to urge him to make the movie, In 1993, it was finally released. Because of Mr. Page's good deed of telling everyone Mr. Schindler's story, we now know how this man resisted the Nazis and saved Jewish lives. Mr. Page once said, "Schindler gave me my life, and I tried to give him immortality."[110]

• During World War I, in 1914, a few days before Christmas, English and German soldiers were fighting between Arras and Neuve Chapelle in Northern France. A wounded elderly British officer lay moaning in No Man's Land, but since he was out in the open, no one dared to go to help him. Fortunately, during a lull in the fighting, a German soldier waved a white flag and was seen by the British soldiers, and then the German soldier took off his pistol belt and ventured out into No Man's Land. A British soldier did the same thing, and they met by the wounded British officer and shook hands. They made a quick truce, and the Germans allowed the British to carry away the wounded British officer. Shortly thereafter, another truce was made to allow the dead to be buried. This truce went on even after the dead were buried and lasted until after Christmas. Fritz Speckhan writes that unfortunately "it was too beautiful to last. Shortly after Christmas special orders came from behind that the shooting was to be resumed. Then at once the truce was over, and the war continued many long and bitter years."[111]

• During the Holocaust, heroes such as Raoul Wallenberg and Oskar Schindler saved thousands of lives. Other people saved fewer lives; for example, Leonard Glinski saved one life in Poland. He noticed a 14-year-old Jewish girl staying in the apartment of his boss. Having a Jew staying in your apartment was dangerous, as helping a Jew was punishable by death. If the Nazis should learn that a Jewish girl was staying there, both the girl and Mr. Glinski's boss would have been killed. Mr. Glinski worked in an underground Resistance group, and he was able to get false papers for the girl, whose name was Alina Pottock, and he helped her go to Vienna, where she survived the war. After the war ended, he reunited her with her uncle and her father. When Mr. Glinski met her at her uncle's home after the war had ended, he says, "She hugged me so hard I almost couldn't breathe." In 1985, she petitioned Yad Vashem, which recognizes the Righteous Among the Nations, to give him a medal. The medal bears a quotation from the Talmud that states that whoever saves one life, it is as if he or she has saved the whole world.[112]

• In 1939, World War II began. Matylda Getter, a Polish nun, was 70 years old, but she did not let that keep her from saving the lives of Jewish children during the Holocaust. She and the sisters of the Family of Mary ran orphanages, and when encouraging the nuns working in the orphanage to save innocent Jewish children, she told the nuns to look into the children's eyes. Often, the children were brought to the orphanage by their parents, who knew that they would be safer there. Later, after the ghettoes were formed, people such as Father Marceli Godlewski, the parish priest of All Saints Church, near the Warsaw Ghetto, smuggled out infants and small children, who were then given false papers identifying them as Catholic. Matylda Getter and the sisters of the Family of Mary saved the lives of at least 500 Jewish children and concealed at least 250 Jewish adults by employing them in their many orphanages. For that, they are recognized as Righteous Among the Nations.[113]

• Swedish diplomat Raoul Wallenberg saved many Jews during the Holocaust by issuing Swedish passports to them. The Nazis respected these passports because Sweden was a neutral country, and the Nazis wished it not to join the side of the Allies. Once, Mr. Wallenberg saw many Jews being loaded onto a train to be taken to a death camp. He stopped, announced who he was, then asked the Jews whether they had Swedish passports. Jews waved papers at him, and Mr. Wallenberg told them that since they were under the protection of the Royal Swedish Legation in Budapest, they could leave the train station. No matter what kind of papers the Jews waved at him, Mr. Wallenberg pretended that the papers were passports, even if they were actually driver's licenses, deportation papers, or eyeglass prescriptions. By doing this, Mr. Wallenberg saved the lives of 300 Jews that day.[114]

• Ira Dutton, aka Brother Joseph, worked among the lepers with Father Damien at Molokai, and he continued his work after Father Damien died. One thing that Brother Joseph requested from President Theodore Roosevelt was that he order a United States battle fleet to sail by Molokai during its around-the-world journey. Brother Joseph felt that the lepers would enjoy the sight of the ships. President Roosevelt sent the battle fleet to Molokai, and as each ship passed Molokai, it dipped its flag in salute. Brother Joseph was not a member of a religious order, and he once declined to become a priest because, he explained, "I am not fit." However, he spent decades working among the lepers, and he once explained why he called himself Brother Joseph although he was a layman: "That is because I want to be a brother to everybody."[115]

• Some Gentiles helped Jews during the Holocaust. Unfortunately, we don't know the full names of some of these Gentiles. For example, in Kreuzen lived a washerwoman named Frau Schmidt, who cleaned the home of a Jewish doctor and his family for years. On *Kristallnacht* the Gestapo arrested the doctor and sent him to the Dachau concentration camp. The doctor's family left their home and hid in a neighbor's home. Each day, Frau Schmidt left a basket of food for them. Another example: Christine and Robert were bakers. When shopkeepers were forbidden by Nazi law to sell to Jews, Christine and Robert continued to bake challah, a bread eaten by many Jews on the Sabbath, and they continued to secretly deliver the challah to Jews for their Shabbos meal.[116]

• In 1943, the Army nurses in the 95th Evacuation Hospital in Capua, Italy, north of Naples, managed to make fudge for Thanksgiving, despite such interruptions as air raids that sent them diving into their foxholes. Nurse Claudine Doyle remembers that during air raids, sometimes a nurse would get out of her foxhole when it seemed safe and run over and stir the fudge. For Christmas that year, the Army nurses decorated a tree, using surgical gloves to make balls. The nurses stuffed the palm section of the glove with gauze, and then they tied all of the fingers of the glove together. Then, to make the glove-ball sparkle, they dipped it into Epsom salts and let it dry. In addition, from tin cans they cut out angels, stars, and Santas.[117]

• While driving one day, boxer Muhammad Ali saw a hungry homeless man being kicked out of a restaurant. He made a U-turn, got out of his car, spoke to the homeless man, and entered the restaurant with him. Mr. Ali then told the restaurant manager, "This man is hungry; he has no place to call home and no food to eat. He is a human being. Since he's worthy enough to occupy space on God's earth, he certainly is worthy enough to eat in this restaurant." He then paid for the hungry man's meal, took him to a hotel and paid for one month's rent, and told the man that he would help him find a job after the man got cleaned up.[118]

• During the Holocaust, the father of Judy Schonfeld Schabes gave much valuable property to some neighbors who were good Christians. The property, Judy says, included "furs, jewelry, silverware, and money," and her father told the Christian neighbors, "Do what you want with this. It's yours." The Schabes family was then taken to Auschwitz on a train that left Beregszasz, Hungary. After surviving the Holocaust, Judy returned to her home and saw the Christian neighbors. They told her that her father "gave this to us, but it's yours." Judy says, "And they gave it all back to me."[119]

• Rabbi Yisroel Salanter once stayed at an inn where he tried to study before going to bed, but he overheard a couple of people in the room adjoining his — the walls were thin. One man was complaining that he was thirsty, and he wanted his companion to go with him to pump water from a well in the dark night. His companion, however, was not thirsty, and would not accompany his fearful friend to the well. Therefore, Rabbi Salanter himself went to the well, pumped some water, gave it to the thirsty man, and then returned to his studies.[120]

• The German army invaded France in 1940, and life for the Jewish Sztrymfman family, who lived in occupied France, changed. Jews endured more and more restrictions, including a restriction that they could not buy food until 5 p.m. Of course, during the war, food was scarce, and little food was available at 5 p.m. Fortunately, Moïshe, the father of the Sztrymfman family, had earlier done a favor for a

Christian neighbor, and the Christian neighbor returned the favor by shopping for food for the Sztrymfmans.[121]

• Some Islamic warriors, including Saladin, captured the Christian warrior Sir Hugh of Tabarie, then released him so that he could gather money to pay for his ransom. He was unable to raise the money, however, so he returned — as he had promised — to be executed. Saladin was so impressed by Sir Hugh's courage and honor that he paid the ransom himself.[122]

• A Zen student saw Yunyan making tea and asked for whom he was making it. Yunyan replied, "For whoever wants to drink it." The student then asked, "But if someone wants tea, can't he make it for himself?" Yunyan replied, "I happen to be here."[123]

• As Muhammad, the prophet of Islam, marched an army to Mecca, he saw a dog that had just given birth. So that the dog and her puppies would not be disturbed, he posted a guard over them.[124]

Holocaust

• What do you do when you can save yourself, but you can't save the ones you love? Janusz Korczak was a famous Jewish writer and radio personality in Warsaw. When the Holocaust came to Poland, he was the head of an orphanage for Jewish children. He was popular with the children, even allowing them to draw on his bald head with crayons. He and the children had to move inside the Warsaw Ghetto, and eventually the Nazis posted signs in the Warsaw Ghetto saying that soon the ghetto would be emptied, and the Jews living there would be moved. Of course, this meant that the Jews would be moved to a concentration camp. Mr. Korczak could have arranged an escape for himself, but how could he arrange an escape for 192 young Jewish orphans? On 6 August 1942, the Nazis ordered Mr. Korczak and the children to walk two miles to a train so they could be moved east. Dressed in their best clothing, Mr. Korczak and the children walked to the train while singing a marching song. There, a Nazi commandant recognized the famous Mr. Korczak and offered him his freedom, but said that he would have to let the children be taken east. Mr. Korczak chose to go with the children. They boarded the train together and were taken to Treblinka, where they died. Mr. Korczak kept a diary. Near the end of his life, he wrote in it, "I never wish anyone ill. I cannot. I don't know how it is done."[125]

• During the Holocaust, Jacques and Germaine Bocquet hid French historian Jules Isaac for one year. When it became too dangerous for him to stay with them, they found him a safer place to stay. He survived the Holocaust and wrote a book titled *Jesus and Israel* about Christian anti-Semitism throughout history. In 1960, he had an audience with Pope John XXIII that led to better relations between Catholics and Jews. Germaine's Catholicism led her to help Jews during the Holocaust; fortunately, she was NOT educated to believe that Jews are "Christ-killers." She almost did not become a Catholic, as her father was not religious. When she was eight years old, her father had her baptized because he thought that it would improve her chances to be well married. He also agreed to the three years of religious training following baptism that changed her life. At the end of the three years, he told her, "At last you are done with all that nonsense!" She replied, "Oh no, Papa, it has only just begun!" While growing up, she used to sneak away from home so that she could attend Mass. After she had become a young woman, when a teacher from a nearby town asked her to shelter a man whom the Gestapo was hunting, she agreed immediately. After all, her religious training had taught her this: "The Jews were for us the people who gave us Jesus."[126]

• During the Holocaust, the Gestapo arrested Malie Piotrskovska and Bronka, her 13-year-old daughter, both Jews, after they were forced to leave their hiding place. Ms. Piotrskovska had false documents that stated that they were Gentiles; however, the Gestapo were suspicious of the documents and asked for verification in the form of a Pole who could vouch that they were really Christians. The only person whom

Ms. Piotrskovska could think of who might help them — at the risk of his own life, since Gentiles who helped Jews were often executed — was Pero, a middle-aged man who worked as a clerk in a hotel in Warsaw. Ms. Piotrskovska worried all night about whether Pero would save her life and the life of her daughter, but in the morning, Pero showed up at the Gestapo offices and swore that Ms. Piotrskovska and her daughter were good Christians. He was able to convince the Gestapo to let the two women go, and he provided shelter for them in his own home.[127]

• Some Jewish survivors of the Holocaust retained a belief in humanity. The father of Aron Hirt-Manheimer was badly mistreated by the Nazis. He had tried to escape from the train that took him to Auschwitz, and he was shot, but survived. He had a number tattooed on his left arm. His son, however, says, "But my father did not give up on humanity. He continued to care about others and refused to judge people collectively." In the 1970s, Aron and his father visited Israel, and their plane stopped at Frankfurt, Germany. Aron looked at the German officials at the airport and whispered to his father in Yiddish, "Damn murderers. We should never have come here." His father replied in Yiddish, "Aron, not all Germans were bad." Aron says, "He tried to pass on to us, to me and my sister Rose, all the best values of Judaism, to be a *mensch* [a good and decent person]." One of the things that the father told his children was this: "You be what you want others to be."[128]

• Oskar Schindler saved over 1,200 Jews during the Holocaust, but when the war was over, he was in danger of being executed. After all, he was a Nazi and a German, and the Russians wanted revenge for the millions of their people who had died during the war. The Jews whom Mr. Schindler had saved wanted to thank and help protect him. They drafted a letter in both Hebrew and German saying that Mr. Schindler had saved many Jews and that he deserved help. They also made a gold ring for him, using the gold teeth — donated — of a man named Szymon Jereth who was among the Jews saved by Mr. Schindler. The gold ring was inscribed with this verse from the Talmud: "He who saves a single life saves the world." That verse also appears on the medal designating Mr. Schindler a Righteous Gentile.[129]

• A single sheet of sacred writing can be a valued possession in times of horror. During the Holocaust, David Weiss Halivni stayed at Gross-Rosen, a work camp in Germany. There he saw a sentry eating a sandwich. What caught his eye was not the sandwich, but what it was wrapped in — a *bletl* or page from a religious text. On his knees, he begged for the page, and the sentry gave it to him. Religious writing was forbidden to Jews in the work camps, but the Jews in Gross-Rosen risked their lives to keep this one sheet of sacred writing, which contained just one paragraph — number 434 — of the laws of Passover. One of the Jews — a Mr. Finkelstein — kept the writing successfully hidden on his person until he died. When he died, the Nazis cremated his body, and the *bletl* was cremated with him.[130]

• Eugene Heimler was angry at the Germans because of the Holocaust, and his anger sometimes made a hate-filled man out of him. He once saw a young German, and he knew that this German was so young that it was impossible for him "to have had any part of the hideous past." But even though this German was nice and had good manners, Mr. Heimler still hated him. However, Mr. Heimler was sorry for hating the German, for he knew that hating was what the Nazis did best. He says, "The feelings I was experiencing were not my own feelings, but theirs. I felt confused. I was doing to him what they had done to me. I was persecuting an innocent man whose only sin was that he happened to be born in Germany."[131]

• The entire nation of Denmark became heroes during World War II because the Danes ferried Denmark's Jewish citizens to safety in Sweden and enabled them to escape deportation to concentration camps. The rescue occurred all over Denmark. In Copenhagen, a bookstore was used as a headquarters for the rescue effort. When a certain poetry book appeared in the bookstore's display window, Jews knew that it was safe to go there. They also knew that once they were in the bookstore they would be taken to safety in Sweden. Sometimes, the owners of the bookstore were so involved in the rescue effort that they became annoyed whenever a real customer wandered into the store and wanted to buy a book.[132]

Husbands and Wives

• Some Rabbis sought Abba Hilkiah to ask him to pray for rain. For a long time, he ignored them — at work, during his journey home, and while he and his family were eating — but then he and his wife went up on the roof of their home, stood at different ends, and prayed for rain, and soon rain clouds came from the direction that his wife was standing and rain began to fall. Abba Hilkiah knew that the Rabbis were puzzled by these things and by other things that he had done, so he explained his behavior to them. The Rabbis had greeted him with "Peace," but because he was working for pay, he did not talk to the Rabbis but instead kept working because he wanted to give his employee a decent day's work for a decent day's pay. When he went home, he carried his cloak on one shoulder and some twigs on the other instead of carrying the twigs in the cloak because he had borrowed the cloak so that he could wear it and not so that he could carry twigs in it. On his way home, he had carried his shoes except for when he had crossed water because on the path he could see what lay before him but he could not see what was in the water. When he had come to bushes with thorns, he had lifted up his pants legs because his flesh could heal but his clothes could not. When he sat down to eat with his family, he did not ask the Rabbis to eat with them because there was not enough food to go around. Seeing that, the Rabbis would have declined to eat, and he didn't want credit for offering them something that he knew that they would decline. When he portioned out the food, he gave the younger son twice as much food as the older son because the older son had eaten at school while the younger son still stayed home all day. Finally, he answered the last question they were thinking: Why did the rain clouds come from the direction where his wife was? Abba Hilkiah said, "Because she is always in the house and gives bread to the poor who come to the house, and the enjoyment of bread is immediate; while I give money, the enjoyment of which is not immediate. Or perhaps it is because of the bandits who were in our neighborhood. I prayed to God that they should die, but she prayed that they should repent."[133]

• Mark Twain and a Mormon once argued over whether the Bible allows polygamy. When the Mormon asked if Mr. Twain could come up with a Bible passage that expressly forbade polygamy, he answered, "That's easy: 'No man can serve two masters.'"[134]

Illness

• When Rabbi Eliezer was ill, Rabbi Yohanan — a very handsome man — visited him. Rabbi Yohanan saw that Rabbi Eliezer was crying, and he asked why he was crying. If Rabbi Eliezer was crying because he had not learned enough Torah, then he should not cry, because he had learned, "Do more, do less, it matters not, so long as one's heart is turned to heaven." If Rabbi Eliezer was crying because he lacked provisions, then he should not cry, because not everyone received provisions both in this world and in the next. If Rabbi Eliezer was crying because he lacked sons, then he should not cry, because Rabbi Yohanan's 10 sons had died. Rabbi Eliezer said, "I am crying over this beauty of yours, which is to wither in the dust." Rabbi Yohanan said, "You are right to cry over that," and the two men cried together.[135]

• An Englishwoman named Sarah learned that she was HIV-positive, and she decided to tell her 16-year-old son. He hugged her like a little boy — he had stopped doing that previously. In addition, he also did little things for her such as taking out the trash or carrying into their home bags from shopping trips. Furthermore, he did things that he did not do before, such as touching her hair. Telling a loved one that you have a life-threatening illness is not easy, but in this case it led to her son expressing his love for her.[136]

Language

• While working for Walt Disney in the 1940s, Ray Kelly heard a joke about a salesman trying to get the Pope to make a change in the wording of the Mass in return for a large amount of money. The salesman wanted the words *Dominus vobiscum* to be replaced with the word "Coca-Cola." Later, Mr. Kelly became a priest, and he admitted that when he first said Mass, every time he said the words *Dominus vobiscum* he thought of the word "Coca-Cola."[137]

• Max Gaines, the father of William M. Gaines of *MAD* magazine fame, used to produce comic books on religious and educational themes; however, the creative process of turning a Biblical story into a comic story with only a limited number of picture panels sometimes tempted him to be profane. For example, he once screamed, "I don't give a d*mn how long it took Moses — I want it in two panels!"[138]

• Father Joseph M. Everson studied Spanish for several months before being assigned to a small church in Peru. Despite his study of Spanish, however, he still had much to learn. At the end of the first wedding he officiated at in Peru, he said (in Spanish): "Go now in peace. This wedding is finished."[139]

Love

• Rabbi Moshe Leib once said that he had learned to love from a peasant. Once he saw two drunken peasants at an inn. One peasant turned to the other and asked, "Do you love me?" The other peasant replied, "Of course I love you." The first peasant then asked, "Do you know what I need? If you really loved me, you would know." According to Rabbi Leib, "To know the needs of other human beings, to feel their joy and to bear the burdens of their sorrow — that is true love."[140]

• Mother Teresa came across a family in India that had 12 children, the youngest of whom was severely handicapped. When Mother Teresa suggested that the handicapped child come to live in one of her homes, the mother started crying and said, "Please, Mother Teresa, don't say that! This child is the greatest gift God has given my family: All our love is showered on her. If you take her away from us, our lives will be without meaning."[141]

• Edith Bunker was a lovable character on *All in the Family*. In fact, the writers of the series used Jesus as a model for her. According to Norman Lear, who produced *All in the Family*, the writers for the character would frequently ask, "In the toughest situations, how would Jesus react?" Mr. Lear says that when Edith met a transvestite in one episode, that's why "she saw the humanity of the person."[142]

• Maya Angelou was active in the Civil Rights Movement, and she met the Reverend Doctor Martin Luther King, Jr., whom she told about Bailey, her brother, who was then in prison after being convicted of selling stolen goods. Dr. King advised her, "Never stop loving him, and never deny him."[143]

Marriage

• According to Rabbi Yossé ben Halaphta, arranging marriages is as difficult for God as it was to part the Sea of Reeds. A Roman matron disbelieved this, and to show that arranging marriages was easy, she matched several of her male and female servants and ordered them to be married. The next morning, however, the servants appeared before her. Some had broken heads; some had broken legs; some had missing eyes. On all sides, she heard, "I can't stand this man!" and "I hate this woman!" The Roman matron then acknowledged that Rabbi Yossé ben Halaphta was absolutely right.[144]

• According to Catherine O'Sullivan, a columnist for the *Tucson Weekly*, "There is no word in the English language as loaded as 'marriage.' It is an inherently religious word." As evidence, she uses her own marriage, which took place in Las Vegas. One witness was a wino, and her flower girl was "a shagged-out hooker." Even so, the marriage ceremony included these words: "Those whom God has joined together, let no man put asunder."[145]

• Early in his radio-broadcasting career, Art Linkletter made an embarrassing mistake. He had asked a young engaged couple if they wished to be married on his radio show the following week. They did, so he announced on the air that the couple would consummate their marriage on his show. His sponsor called to inform Mr. Linkletter that the marriage ceremony and the consummation of a marriage are two separate events.[146]

• A BBC announcer once asked Mother Teresa if it was easier for her to help other people because she wasn't married. "This is not true. I am married, too," she replied, displaying the ring that symbolized her marriage to Christ. Mother Teresa added, "And he can be very difficult sometimes."[147]

• Msgr. Charles Dollen once officiated at a wedding where the nervous groom botched the vows so badly that afterward the bride, truly concerned, asked if she was really married. Msgr. Dollen replied, "Yes, so long as you never get sick."[148]

• Rabbi Malcolm Schwartz of Los Angeles had a good sense of humor. When a man asked for his daughter's hand in marriage, he replied, "That's all right with me, son, just so long as you take the one that's always in my pocket!"[149]

Chapter 4: From Miracles to Prejudice

Miracles

• God wants intelligent, independent followers. Rabbi Eliezer made several arguments, but the other Rabbis did not agree with his arguments. Rabbi Eliezer said, "If my arguments are correct, may that tree prove it." The tree moved several feet in the earth, but the other Rabbis said, "A tree proves nothing." Rabbi Eliezer said, "If my arguments are correct, may that stream of water prove it." The stream of water reversed itself and flowed up a hill, but the other Rabbis said, "A stream of water proves nothing." Rabbi Eliezer said, "If my arguments are correct, may the walls of the House of Study prove it." The walls of the House of Study immediately bent inwards, but the other Rabbis said, "The walls of the House of Study prove nothing." Rabbi Eliezer said, "If my arguments are correct, may Heaven prove it." A voice from Heaven proclaimed that the arguments of Rabbi Eliezer were correct. However, Rabbi Joshua quoted Deuteronomy 30:12: "It is not in the heavens." Explaining why Rabbi Joshua said this, Rabbi Jeremiah said, "He meant that since the Torah has been given already on Mount Sinai, we do not pay attention to a heavenly voice, for Thou hast written in Thy Torah, 'Decide according to the majority" (Exodus 23:2). So how did God react to the result of this discussion in which a majority opinion (in accordance with the Torah) bested miracles? Rabbi Nathan met and asked the Prophet Elijah exactly that question. Elijah said, "He was laughing, and saying, 'My children have defeated me. My children have defeated me.'" God gave His children the Torah, and God wants His children to become mature. In this story, Humankind's understanding of what makes a good argument wins out over the miracles, yet the existence of the miracles is not disputed.[150]

• According to John, Jesus healed a man of blindness by spitting on the ground, mixing up mud, putting the mud on the blind man's eyes, and then telling him to wash it off in the Pool of Siloam. Modern archaeologists have discovered this pool, which is located in the Jerusalem suburb of Siloam, and from its dimensions, they know that the pool of Siloam was a place of ritual purification. This sheds light on Jesus' miracle. Blind people could not enter the Temple, so by curing the blind man and at the same time sending him to a place of ritual purification, Jesus was making it possible for the man to finally be able to worship at the Temple.[151]

• Bahlool the wise fool once announced that he was a prophet. Of course, his countrymen were skeptical, so Bahlool told them that a fair test that he really was a prophet would be if he could read their minds. His countrymen agreed that if he could read their minds that this would prove that Bahlool was in fact a prophet. Bahlool then said, "You are thinking that I am a fake and not a prophet at all, aren't you?"[152]

• Brazilian author Paulo Coelho is aware that Jesus' first miracle — turning water into superb wine at a wedding celebration when the wine has run out — is not politically correct. However, he does think that the miracle is significant. He believes that the miracle is a way for Jesus to say, "[L]ook, although I will go through moments of great pain, the way is the way of joy and not of pain."[153]

Money

• Proper pride exists, but at times one must humble oneself to help other people. Abbé Pierre founded the Emmaus movement, which seeks to help the homeless and poor. Abbé Pierre was a member of the Resistance in World War II, and after the war he worked to help the homeless and the hungry in Paris. At one point, he needed money to feed the hungry, so he dressed in an old jacket, on the front of which he put the seven medals he had won for his work in the war, then he went to a fashionable area of Paris with many good (and expensive) restaurants, and he begged for money to feed the hungry. Another way that people in Emmaus made money was through rag-picking — going through trash to find things to sell. Abbé Pierre did find another, more interesting way to make money for the Emmaus movement. He went on a popular radio quiz show named "Double or Nothing." Give the right answer and double your money, or give the wrong answer and lose all of your money. Abbé Pierre gave enough right answers that he won 250,000 francs for the poor.[154]

• In the old days, many Protestants considered it a sin to spend money on the Sabbath. (Orthodox Jews still think it is a sin to carry money on the Sabbath.) Alyene Porter's father was a Texas preacher in the early part of the 20th century, and he never spent money on the Sabbath. Instead, he planned ahead, buying feed for his horse, and later, gasoline for his car on Saturday. He even ordered milk for his family to be delivered on Saturday evening, so he wouldn't have to buy any on the Sabbath. Once, he woke early and found that the milk he had ordered to be delivered by a farmer on Saturday evening was being delivered on Sunday morning. He immediately telephoned the farmer's wife and said, "Mrs. Brown, I'm sorry. We don't buy milk on Sunday." She replied, "But Brother Porter, unfortunately the cows give milk on Sunday." He answered, "Yes — unfortunately."[155]

• A wealthy sultan once visited a sheikh who had many spiritual followers. The sultan was impressed by the wisdom of the sheikh and began to attend his gatherings, where he was liberal with gifts. Finally, the sultan told the sheikh that he would give him anything he asked for. The sheikh asked the sultan to leave because the sheikh's followers used to come to the gatherings because of their respect for God, but now they attended the gatherings so they could receive a gift from the sultan. The sheikh told the sultan, "We are not spiritually advanced enough to handle your presence."[156]

• A rich miser came to see a Rabbi for advice. The Rabbi asked the miser to look out a window and to tell him what he saw. The miser answered, "People." The Rabbi then asked the miser to look in a mirror and to tell him what he saw. The miser answered, "Myself." The Rabbi then pointed out that both the mirror and the window consisted of glass. However, to the glass of the mirror was added a little silver, and as soon as the silver was added, the miser stopped seeing other people and saw only himself.[157]

• Sometimes selfishness doesn't pay. A woman owned a Buddha that was covered with beautiful gold foil. She once stayed at a temple where there were many other Buddhas, and when she burned incense for her Buddha, she didn't want to share the scent with the other Buddhas, so she used a funnel to make sure that the smoke from the incense went directly to the nose of her Buddha. After a few times of her doing this, however, people started to laugh at her Buddha — its nose was covered with black soot.[158]

• In the summer of 1916, during World War I, some German prisoners of war in France were allowed to attend a French church. Many French churches were without pews, and such was the case in this French church, located in Montagny. However, hassocks (cushions) were available at a price. An old French woman was in charge of distributing the hassocks, and she gave one to each German soldier. When the Germans attempted to pay for the hassocks, she said simply, "Soldiers don't pay."[159]

• A minister played golf with a man who said that his average was the same as the minister's, but who was actually a hustler. They bet $1 per hole to make the game interesting, and the hustler won all 18 holes. Knowing that he had been cheated, the minister handed over the money, then asked the hustler where he lived. The hustler asked, "Why do you want to know that?" The minister replied, "I thought that I'd go over and perform a marriage ceremony for your mother and father."[160]

• A man once asked Rabbi Hillel a series of stupid questions, and Rabbi Hillel answered each question patiently, using the Torah as his source of wisdom. Finally, the man admitted that he had made a bet that he could make Rabbi Hillel angry and that he had lost the bet. Rabbi Hillel asked how much the man had bet. Hearing the answer,

Rabbi Hillel said, "You may have lost 20 dinars, but you have gained something of far greater worth: a taste of the Torah."[161]

• When Sarah Bernhardt toured the United States, she was often accused of appearing in immoral plays, and often clergymen gave her valuable publicity by denouncing her plays. Once, Ms. Bernhardt sent the Bishop of Chicago a check and a note: "Your Excellency, I am accustomed when I bring an attraction to town, to spend $400 on advertising. As you have done half the advertising for me, I herewith enclose $200 for your parish."[162]

• During the Great Depression, Truett "Rip" Sewell was a teenager who traveled with his father, a salesman — Rip did the driving. One Sunday, Rip asked his father for a dime so he could visit a candy store that was located next to a Methodist church. However, his father showed him three pennies and said, "I only have these, and I would like to put them in the offering basket." Later, Rip became a pitcher for the Pittsburgh Pirates.[163]

• On Purim, rich Jews give gifts to the poor. One Purim, Rabbi Joseph Saul Nathanson of Lemberg saw a rich man reading the Talmud in the House of Study. The Rabbi snatched the book out of the rich man's hands and said, "On Purim, your place is not to study the Talmud. On Purim, your place is to stay at home before a plate full of money and give generously to the poor who come to see you."[164]

• Even as a boy, the future Rabbi Naphtali of Ropshitz (1760-1827) was very intelligent. Once an adult said to him, "Naphtali, I'll give you a gold coin if you can tell where God is to found." Naphtali answered, "I'll give you two gold coins if you can tell me where God is not to be found."[165]

• Clara Null once lived in a small town that had one bank and three churches. One Monday morning, the bank called all three churches and asked them to bring in their Sunday collections — the bank had run out of $1 bills.[166]

Music

• As part of their preparation for the High Holy Days, Mary Blye Howe and other members of her synagogue would gather at a nearby lake. There they listened to their Rabbis teach about the significance of the High Holy Days, and they said prayers. After reflection, each member of the synagogue threw crumbs that symbolized his or her shortcomings into the lake. As a group, the members of the synagogue then crossed a bridge to symbolize the crossing from the old year to the new year. Barry Diamond, a charismatic Rabbi at the synagogue, played music as the members crossed the bridge. To inject some humor following a solemn time, he would sometimes play a little of Led Zeppelin's "Stairway to Heaven," then say, "Oops! Wrong bridge!"[167]

• Early in her career, gospel singer Mahalia Jackson often sang in Chicago churches, but sometimes her down-South-style singing was not appreciated. One pastor became angry and told Mahalia to take that "jazz" she was singing out of his church. Mahalia told him, "This is the way we sing down South! I been singing this way all my life in church! If it's undignified, it's what the Bible told me to do!" The Bible passage she had in mind was from Psalm 47: "Oh, clap your hands, all ye people! Shout unto the Lord with the voice of a trumpet!"[168]

Names

• When Agnes Gonxha Bojaxhiu decided to become a nun, Lazar, her brother, who had become an army officer for King Zog I of Albania, worried about whether she had made the right choice. She told him, "You will serve a king of two million people; I will serve the King of the whole world." Years later, when his sister Agnes had become known to the world as Mother Teresa, he knew that she had made the right decision. He admitted, "It can be truly said that she is a commandant of a unit or an entire fleet. Her strength of will is unbelievable, like our mother's."[169]

• In the old days, people were frequently given names based on scripture. For example, one man was named "If Christ Had Not Died for Thee Thou Hadst Been Damned Barebone." He became a theologian and was called Dr. Damned Barebone.[170]

• Pope John XXIII, whose name was Angelo Roncalli before he became Pope, asked a boy his name. The boy replied, "Arcangelo." "Oh, poor me," the Pope said. "I'm just plain Angelo."[171]

Paradise

• One should tell the truth, even when telling the truth means admitting that you are guilty. Rabbi Elimelech of Lyzhansk believed in a merciful God Who is also a judge. He said that on the Day of Judgment, God would ask him some questions. God would ask, "Have you been as just and as righteous as you ought to have been? Have you been as charitable as you ought to have been? Have you studied sacred writings as much as you should have? Have you prayed as much as you should have?" To each of these questions, Rabbi Elimelech would answer with the truth: "No." However, Rabbi Elimelech believed that God, Who is merciful, would then say, "Elimelech, you have spoken the truth. For this alone, you will have a share in the World to Come."[172]

• According to a traditional story, a Rabbi once asked the prophet Elijah to look over a crowd and point out those people who were destined for Paradise. Elijah did so and picked out two jesters. Because the jesters were not noted for being religious, the Rabbi asked why they were destined for Paradise. Elijah replied that the job of a jester is to bring laughter to people who were hurting, and this job made them worthy of a place in Paradise.[173]

Pesach

• One Pesach, Rabbi Levi Itzhak of Berdichev walked among his neighbors, asking, "Have you any leaven in your home?" Each time, he received the answer that not a crumb of leaven was to be found in any Jew's home. The good Rabbi then asked if anyone had any contraband silk that had been forbidden by the Czar. Immediately, the answer came back that such silk was readily available. The good Rabbi then prayed, "The Russian Czar is powerful and has armed guards everywhere, and yet his people disregard his commandment and smuggle contraband items. But You have no armed guards. You have only ordained in the Torah, 'Seven days shalt there be no leaven found in your houses.' Yet see how observant Jews are of Your commandment! Truly Israel is a unique people on Earth!"[174]

Politics

• USA President Lyndon Johnson liked exaggerated Texas humor. West German chancellor Ludwig Erhard once said to President Johnson, "I understand you were born in a log cabin, Mr. President." President Johnson replied, "No, Mr. Chancellor, I was born in a manger."[175]

• At a rally, Boston mayor Jim Curley was heckled by a man who yelled, "I wouldn't vote for you even if you were Saint Peter." Mr. Curley replied, "If I were Saint Peter, you wouldn't even be in my district."[176]

Prayer

• In December 1848, a frail Southern gentleman attended by a black male slave boarded a train. The Southern gentleman's right arm and face were bandaged, and when other passengers spoke to him, he did not answer, which made the other passengers conclude that he was deaf. Because the Southern gentleman and his slave had bought train tickets to Philadelphia, Pennsylvania, a state without slavery, this aroused the suspicions of an officer, who wanted to know why they were going to Pennsylvania. However, the other passengers protested at the questioning of an invalid, so the officer let the Southern gentleman and his slave stay on the train. In Philadelphia, the truth became known. The frail Southern gentleman and his slave were actually William and Ellen Craft, a married slave couple who had just used an effective disguise to escape from slavery and gain their freedom. Ellen's skin was light enough for her to pass for white; however, no white woman would travel alone with a slave, so she needed to disguise herself as a man. To disguise her lack of a beard, her face was bandaged.

She didn't know how to read or write, hence her hand was bandaged so that no one would ask her to write something. In their book *Running a Thousand Miles for Freedom*, the Crafts wrote that the day they reached Philadelphia, they stayed at the boardinghouse of an abolitionist, knelt on the floor, "and poured out our heartfelt gratitude to God, for his goodness in enabling us to overcome so many perilous difficulties, in escaping out of the jaws of the wicked."[177]

• Muslims say five daily prayers. This may seem like a lot to non-Muslims, but the number of daily prayers could have been much higher. The angel Gabriel visited the prophet Muhammad in Mecca and took him first to Jerusalem and then to the heavens, where Muhammad crossed the threshold leading to the Divine Presence. When Muhammad left to return to Earth, he left with instructions about daily prayers, of which there were 50. However, on his way back to Earth Muhammad met Moses, who advised him to return and cross the threshold again into the Divine Presence and ask for a reduction in the number of daily prayers. This happened a number of times, and when Muhammad finally returned to Earth, the number of obligatory daily prayers had been reduced to five, which Muslims still say each day.[178]

• Carmen Murguia of Milwaukee, Wisconsin, knew that she was a lesbian at age seven! No, this was not a phase she was going through. At age 40, she is still a lesbian. Because she is Catholic, she visited a church and prayed to Our Lady of Guadalupe and to God, saying, "You made me be female. You made me brown. Now I've discovered I like girls, too. It's going to be a long road, so you better take good care of me. Amen." At age 40, Ms. Murguia is surprised that she knew to say that particular prayer at age seven, "Where did that come from? I was only seven. Gay and lesbian children have so much insight and love, but they also need a lot of love, too." [179]

• When he was a young boy, one of Mark Twain's prayers was answered. In church he had heard in a sermon that God answered prayers, and so he put that information to the test. One of his schoolmates, Margaret Kooneman, brought gingerbread to school each day as part of her lunch, and since young Mark liked gingerbread, at school one day he prayed for gingerbread. Looking up after his prayer, he saw young Margaret's gingerbread, and he saw that young Margaret had her back turned toward the gingerbread. Mr. Twain later reflected in his *Autobiography*, "In all my life I believe I never enjoyed an answer to prayer more than I enjoyed that one."[180]

• The Earl of Sandwich is well known for having invented the sandwich. He was also an atheist who was known for his blasphemy as well as for his gambling. Occasionally, he herded cows and sheep into the chapel on his property and preached to them a mock sermon. He also kept a baboon that he called his chaplain. Once, he held a dinner party, among whose guests were a clergyman and his wife. The Earl asked the baboon to say grace, to which the clergyman replied, "My lord, I had intended performing this duty myself, not knowing until now that you had so close a relative in holy orders."[181]

• Country comedian Jerry Clower wore a piece of jewelry that he had specially made up — it has both a Christian cross and a Jewish Star of David. Mr. Clower explained, "I do a lot of shows with people who wear the Star of David and a lot of shows with people who wear the cross. I believe what the Bible says about both of them." The piece of jewelry also includes a diamond. When asked about the diamond, Mr. Clower saed, "That represents the self-centeredness and hillbilly in me. And I'm trying to overcome it. Pray for me."[182]

• In 1980, Elie Wiesel and other humanitarians went to Southeast Asia with supplies, including medicine and food, intended to help Cambodian refugees. However, border guards at the Thailand-Cambodia border stopped them from delivering the supplies. Mr. Wiesel then began to recite the Kaddish, the prayer for the dead, for his father, who had died at Buchenwald 35 years previously. The prayer was also appropriate for the many people who died because of famine and war due to Pol Pot.[183]

• While Joe Lewis was training for a heavyweight champion bout back in the days when prices were a lot lower than they are now, he received a letter from a pastor telling him that the pastor's congregation would be gathering at the church and praying for him during the fight. The pastor added, "If it rains while we're praying for you, we may get a little wet. It would cost $27.50 to fix the roof."[184]

• In the late 1960s, students tended to have long hair, and university administrators tended to have short hair. During a time of unrest, a preacher prayed before a meeting of students and university administrators, saying, "O God, bless all those here with long hair, and all those here with short hair, and all those here with no hair, and help them to love each other."[185]

• Republican Steven Derounian of New York strongly supported prayer in school. During a speech, he once stated, "The right to pray is as sacred as the mother's right to nurse a child." A female opponent then asked, "In school?" (In my opinion, lots of silent prayer exists in school — especially at test time.)[186]

• When Quaker humorist Tom Mullen went into a hospital for an operation, he was visited by many people who prayed for him. This allowed him to discover that some visitors do strange things while praying for ill people. For example, one visitor had the habit of praying while squeezing and wiggling Mr. Mullen's big toe.[187]

• At Auschwitz, Rabbi Dovid Goldwasser said prayers in Hebrew for the Jews who had lost their lives there. When he finished praying, he noticed that a group of non-Jews had been standing nearby, listening to his prayer. Although they did not understand a word of Hebrew, tears were streaming down their faces.[188]

• A little girl was sent to bed just as a party for her parents' friends was beginning. Her mother said, "Say good night to all our guests, and don't forget to say your prayers." "Okay," the little girl said. "Anybody need anything?"[189]

Preachers

• David Frost's father was a fine preacher, in part because of an accident that happened to David Frost's grandmother. Mr. Frost's grandmother was riding in a carriage that turned over, so she threw herself across her baby to protect it. The baby was fine, but because of the accident, she became deaf. Therefore, as the baby — Mr. Frost's father — was growing up, he enunciated everything very clearly so his mother (Mr. Frost's grandmother) could read his lips. This enunciation practice paid off when he became a preacher. Mr. Frost says, "My father up in the pulpit is now the greatest preacher I've ever heard. He pronounces and enunciates so properly. Why? Because of a disability of his mother. God took that and used it so my father would be a better preacher."[190]

• Rod Parker was the executive producer of the TV sitcom *Maude*, which often did episodes on such controversial topics as abortion — in fact, the title character gets an abortion. His wife came from Shenandoah, Pennsylvania, and her mother was proud that her daughter had married a Hollywood producer. The local newspaper interviewed the mother, so everybody knew whom her daughter had married. Unfortunately, when she went to church that Sunday, the preacher gave a sermon about how "those terrible people on *Maude* were murderers." Of course, a lot of people in the congregation started staring at her.[191]

• Quaker humorist Tom Mullen once heard a preacher talk about people who try to say "Yes," but instead constantly say, "Yes, but ...." The preacher said, "We are always saying, 'Yes, but ....' Again and again we, too, fall back on our buts."[192]

Prejudice

• The highly qualified eye specialist Dr. Max Mandelstamm was considered for a professorship at the University of Kiev, but he was rejected solely because he was a Jew. Therefore, he sent the university this letter by messenger: "I respectfully recommend the bearer of this letter to the Chair of Ophthalmology at the university. He is not an eye specialist, but he answers to your requirements. He is a Christian, and he has for years been my dependable furnace-tender."[193]

• Comedian Phil Baker was Jewish — his real last name was Shapiro. As a guest of a member, he was golfing at a course in Westchester County when the assistant manager of the golf course walked over to him and told him that he was playing in a restricted club (meaning, no Jews allowed) and would have to leave. Mr. Baker replied, "Couldn't I play just nine holes? My wife's a Gentile."[194]

• At one time, Morris K. Udall's World War II roommate, whose name was Stanley Kurz, offered to make Mr. Udall an "honorary Jew." Flattered, he asked what perks came with the honor, and Mr. Kurz replied, "Two thousand years of persecution — retroactive."[195]

Chapter 5: From Problem-Solving to Zen

Problem-Solving

- Four brothers argued over their inheritance when their father died, and each brother argued that he deserved more of their father's wealth than the other brothers. After all, each brother had worked hard on the father's property, doing his share of the work on the farm and using his own particular talent in his work. One brother took care of the growing of crops, one brother took care of maintaining the buildings, one brother took care of the cattle, and one brother took care of the other animals. Shakyamuni Buddha heard of the brothers' disagreement, and so he called all the brothers to him and told them a story about an ill king who needed lion's milk to be healed. The king sent out announcements that whoever brought him lion's milk would be rewarded with a marriage to one of the king's daughters and with kingship over a country of his own. A hunter heard the announcement and set out to get lion's milk. He drugged some meat and set it out so that any lion that ate the meat would go to sleep. Just as the hunter had planned, a lion ate the meat and fell asleep, and the hunter was able to milk the lion. The hunter then began to journey to the king. It was a long journey, and the hunter got tired and rested, falling asleep. While he was asleep, he dreamed that the parts of his body were arguing over who deserved the most credit for obtaining the lion's milk. His legs argued that they had done the walking to get to the lion and to take the lion's milk to the king, and so they deserved the most credit. His arms argued that they had done the milking, and so they deserved the most credit. His ears argued that they had heard the king's proclamation, and so they deserved the most credit. His eyes argued that without sight, drugging and milking the lion and taking the lion's milk to the palace would have been impossible, and so they deserved the most credit. Just then, the hunter awoke, and he told himself that all of the parts of his body had done their jobs well and so all the parts of his body deserved an equal part in the reward that the hunter would receive from the king for getting lion's milk. After hearing the Buddha's story, the brothers resolved to split the inheritance equally and to continue to work together on the farm.[196]

• An innkeeper joined a band of robbers and set up guests to be robbed by telling them at night that a caravan had passed and that they should join it so they would not be robbed. When the guests left the inn in hopes of catching up with the caravan, the robbers fell upon them and took their money and goods. Rabbi Meir was a guest at that inn one night, and the innkeeper woke him up to tell him to catch up with the caravan. However, Rabbi Meir explained that it was night and the night was populated with robbers. The innkeeper insisted that Rabbi Meir would be safe in the caravan, so Rabbi Meir then explained that he could not leave without his brother Ki Tov, adding, "When you find Ki Tov, who is now in the synagogue, I will leave." The innkeeper went to the synagogue, searching for Ki Tov, while Rabbi Meir stayed in bed and slept. In the morning, when it was light, Rabbi Meir left the inn but met the innkeeper, who complained, "I called all night for your brother, but no one answered." Rabbi Meir replied, "In the Torah, God calls the light *Ki Tov*, which means "it is good." One always finds light in the synagogue, for the Torah is there, and it guides our way. And now that it is morning — and safe — one finds light everywhere."[197]

• Two women came to Rabbi Hirschele Orenstein of Brisk (Brest-Litovsk) with a dispute over a basket of clothing. The two women were neighbors, and each woman accused the other of taking clothing from her clothesline. The Rabbi talked to the two women, but he was unable to tell which woman was lying. Therefore, he asked the women to leave the basket of disputed clothing with him, then leave and come back in an hour. While the women were gone, he asked his wife to mix some of her clothing with the clothing in the basket. When the two women returned in an hour, he did not tell the women what he had done, but he asked the first woman to go through the clothing and pick out what was hers. The woman quickly made two piles of clothing: one pile contained the clothing of the Rabbi's wife. The Rabbi then asked the other woman to go through the clothing and pick out what was hers. This woman said, "It is all mine." The Rabbi replied, "In that case, none of it is yours."[198]

• Joe Garagiola had to solve an unusual problem while speaking to a scholar-athlete group in St. Louis. The maitre d' told him the hotel was on fire, and the fire department wanted the ballroom to be evacuated. Mr. Garagiola announced to the crowd, "Don't be alarmed, but I've just been told to ask you to please leave the ballroom. Everything is under control, but please start filing out through the south door." Unfortunately, because Mr. Garagiola is known for his comedy, everyone laughed and no one moved. He then announced, "This is no joke. There's a fire in the hotel, and the fire department has asked us to vacate the room." Same result. So Mr. Garagiola tried a third time, "This is not a joke. If you want to stay here, you can, but I'm grabbing those nuns seated by the exit and leading them out because my mother would never forgive me if something happened to them." This worked, as everyone followed Mr. Garagiola and the nuns out of the room.[199]

• Ed Brown, a priest and cook at the Tassajara Zen Mountain Center[1] (and Hot Springs) in California, and Purple Gene have been friends for a long time. One of Purple Gene's favorite stories about Ed is about the early, rigorous days of monastic training at Tassajara when students were very hungry as they adjusted to the strict vegetarian diet. Sometimes, students would raid the kitchen at night, so Ed was appointed to stop them. He used to sit on top of the refrigerator, with his legs held in lotus position and his hands clutching two knives. When a student attempted to raid the kitchen, Ed would scare them. However, soon a better solution for the problem was found. Founding Abbot Suzuki Roshi advised, "Take the lock off your mind — put it on the door!"[200]

---

1.   http://www.sfzc.org/tassajara/

• At one time, the Spiceland Quarterly Meeting and the Walnut Ridge Quarterly Meeting in Indiana were one meeting, and some Quakers had to travel a long distance to attend the meeting. Of course, it was the custom of local Quakers to invite to dinner those Quakers who had traveled long distances to attend the meeting. Once, a Quaker who had traveled a long distance had not received an invitation, so he approached a local Quaker and said, "Will thee go home with me for dinner?" The local Friend asked, "Where does thee live?" On hearing the answer — "At Carthage, only about 13 miles from here" (a long distance, before modern transportation) — the local Friend took the hint and invited the other man to come home with him to dinner.[201]

• John Neumann (1811-1860), the first American bishop to be canonized as a saint, strongly supported education. When he was Bishop of Philadelphia, he wished for the priests to start parochial schools. Most did, eagerly and happily, but a few resisted, including one who claimed, "It is impossible just now." The bishop wrote the priest, "If it is impossible for you to establish a school, I shall look for another to fill your place. He will perhaps find it possible to secure a Christian education for the children of this parish." The priest immediately reconsidered and immediately started a school. The first day that enrollment was open, 1,000 pupils enrolled.[202]

• Comedian Phyllis Diller's mother was a problem-solver. At the Methodist church the family attended, small children grew fretful during the sermon in adult church. How to solve this problem? Her mother came up with the idea of junior church, which took place downstairs at the church, where Sunday School was held, and which presented much the same content as the adult sermon did — but in a form simple enough for children to understand. Phyllis calls this idea "brilliant."[203]

• Baseball player Jay Kirke once missed a signal in the ninth inning and lost a game for his Louisville team in the American Association. Manager Joe McCarthy was plenty steamed and ordered Mr. Kirke to report to him in the clubhouse later. Mr. Kirke was no fool. He knew that Mr. McCarthy was going to unload a heaping helping of torrential abuse upon his head, so when he arrived at the clubhouse, he brought someone with him — a priest. Mr. Kirke told the priest, "Come on in, Father. I want you to meet a friend of mine."[204]

• The government of the USSR was officially atheist, and the practice of religion was greatly discouraged. In Armenia, whose citizens were Christian, religious people got around the ban on Christmas by giving gifts on New Year's Day. The authorities allowed these gifts because New Year's Day is not a religious holiday. Despite the anti-religious authorities, many Armenians continued to make their traditional Easter eggs.[205]

• Kovno had a building known as the *hekdesh*, which was owned by the community and used as a place for the poor to sleep. Through neglect, the building had fallen into disrepair. R' Yisrael Salanter knew that action needed to be taken to repair the building, so he slept there one night. The next day, word spread that the good Rabbi had slept in the *hekdesh*, and immediately plans were made to repair it.[206]

• Zen master Kansan became the leader of an abbacy at a distant temple. After traveling to the temple, he discovered that it was located in an area with much alcoholism. In fact, alcohol was even served in the temple. Immediately, Kansan smashed every wine jar, every ashtray, and every serving table in the temple. Afterward, guests to the temple were served tea.[207]

• The evangelist D.L. Moody was a problem-solver. During a revival, a man began a prayer that went on and on and on, boring everyone. Finally, Mr. Moody stood up and said, "While our brother finishes his prayer, let's sing a hymn." The audience quickly began singing a hymn, and our brother quickly said "Amen."[208]

Public Speaking

• Sometimes, the introductions of public speakers can drag on much too long. In Johannesburg, South Africa, speaker Maurice

Samuel had to wait for over 40 minutes as Rabbi Rome went on and on in his introduction of a weary Mr. Samuel, who had just finished a long flight. Finally, the introduction completed, Mr. Samuel rose and said, "Ladies and gentlemen, while Rome was fiddling, I was burning."[209]

• Abby Kelley, a Quaker, spoke often to advocate the abolition of slavery. Once, a man in the audience argued against abolition, saying that human history showed that slavery had always existed. He demanded, "When did slavery [begin]? How long has it existed?" Ms. Kelley replied, "About as long as murder," and the audience applauded her answer.[210]

Rescuers

• Pastor André Trocmé was the spiritual leader of Le Chambon, a French village whose inhabitants helped save 5,000 strangers, most of them Jews, during the Holocaust. Several other villages in the area, the Plateau Vivarais-Lignan in France's Laute-Loire region, helped in the rescue. One reason for this help was the history of the villages in the Plateau Vivarais-Lignan, which was a Protestant area surrounded by a larger Catholic area. The Protestant inhabitants knew how it felt to be discriminated against because of their religion, and therefore they came to the aid of other people who were discriminated against because of their religion. Another reason for this help was Pastor Trocmé, who preached that the Jews were the people of God. Many of the Jews the French in this area helped were surprised at how accepting the French people were. For example, one Jewish woman came to a farm to buy eggs. The farmer's wife asked if she was Jewish. Hearing an affirmative answer, the farmer's wife turned and shouted. The Jewish woman was at first about to flee, but she was relieved to hear that the farmer's wife was simply calling to her husband to come and see one of the people of God. Because of their saving of 5,000 lives during the Holocaust, all of the inhabitants of the Plateau Vivarais-Lignan were recognized as Righteous Among the Nations.[211]

• Some Catholic priests were rescuers of Jews during the Holocaust. Bernard and Charles Rotmil were brothers who became hidden children of the Holocaust. After their father was taken to Auschwitz, they traveled from France to Louvain, Belgium. In Louvain, they went to a Catholic monastery, where Father Bruno helped them. Bernard entered a camp for boys, and Charles, who was too young for the camp, hid with a farm family. Both boys were very impressed by Father Bruno, and they asked him to baptize them. However, Father Bruno knew that the boys were Jewish, and he declined to baptize them because he did not have the permission of their parents. The two boys survived the Holocaust, but the rest of their family died.[212]

Sabbath

• Modern technology has sometimes created dilemmas for Jews who wish to observe the Sabbath. For example, is it permissible to ride the elevator on the Sabbath and on holy days? Dr. Solomon Schechter, an early president of the Jewish Theological Seminary, lived in an apartment building — on the ninth floor. Sometimes, he invited his students to share a Sabbath meal with him at his home. When that happened, he took the elevator — but he told his young, vigorous students to take the stairs. Some Jews believe that it is OK to take the elevator on the Sabbath and on holy days, but only as long as they don't have to press any buttons. Therefore, in some homes for the Jewish aged, the elevators automatically stop at every floor on the Sabbath and on holy days.[213]

• Elijah, the Gaon of Wilna, was an outstanding Rabbi. Once he urged a Jew of his community to undertake a journey on behalf on some fellow Jews who were facing persecution by the government. The Jew's mission was a success, and he saved many Jews from persecution, but because of his mission he was unable to properly observe the Sabbath. Feeling guilty, he asked Rabbi Elijah what he should do for repentance. Rabbi Elijah told him, "Let's make an exchange. I will give you the reward of a Sabbath that I properly observed if you will give me the reward of the Sabbath that you did not properly observe."[214]

• An emperor once asked Rabbi Joshua Ben Hananiah why Jewish food tasted so good on the Sabbath. Rabbi Joshua replied that the food tasted so good because the Jews used a special spice. When the emperor asked for some of the special spice, Rabbi Joshua answered, "This spice is available only to those who observe the day of rest, for the spice is the Sabbath itself."[215]

Saints

• Social activist Dorothy Day may become a saint. She worked for social justice using nonviolent resistance and co-founded in 1933 the periodical *Catholic Worker* to educate people. Robert Coles, a psychiatrist and author, once went to the Bowery so he could meet her. When he found her, she was talking to a woman who was drunk. Eventually, Ms. Day asked Mr. Coles, "Which one of us do you wish to talk to?" Mr. Coles believes that Ms. Day's prayers saved his wife from an illness that could have killed her. If this is a miracle, she has met one more requirement for being canonized.[216]

• Sufi master Shemsu-'d-Din, aka Shems, tutored a very stupid but very handsome prince. He was so successful that the prince succeeded in memorizing the entire Quran. The prince's accomplishment made people suspect that his tutor was a saint, so Shems slipped away quietly and went elsewhere.[217]

Scripture

• In 1941, people were worried about the war and about foreign spies. In addition, people were concerned about relieving human misery. Four American Quakers journeyed to England to see about undertaking some relief efforts. However, one of the Quakers was detained under suspicion of being a foreign spy when a book written in a foreign language and a map of the Mediterranean on which had been drawn lines was found in his possession. Fortunately, the matter was quickly cleared up. The book was a Greek New Testament, and the map showed the wanderings of St. Paul. The items were returned to Bible scholar Henry Cadbury, and he continued his relief efforts.[218]

• Buddhists attempt to get rid of the ego. The Buddha taught, but he did not write down his sayings. Only after more than 400 years after the Buddha died did some monks in Sri Lanka decide to write down the Buddha's sayings. Only one monk had memorized the Buddha's entire sayings, and he was arrogant about his deed. Thich Nhat Hanh, a Vietnamese Buddhist monk, says, "When we hear this, we feel a little uneasy knowing that an arrogant monk may not have been the best vehicle to transmit the teachings of the Buddha."[219]

Sermons

• Bishop Roberts, an early Methodist, was once asked by a man about Bishop Soule and Dr. Emory, both of whom he knew well and thought highly of. The man then asked, "There was another, an old man, who preached not long since in our place; I think they called him Bishop Roberts; they say he is a most excellent man, but no great preacher — do you know him?" Bishop Roberts was not a man of sinful pride. He replied, "I have been acquainted with him for a good many years; I believe the old man is honest and tries to do the best he can, but you are right — he's not much of a preacher."[220]

• Dodger co-owner Branch Rickey knew Dr. Norman Vincent Peale, who frequently visited Ebbets Field. Mr. Rickey knew baseball, and he liked to contribute sermon ideas to Dr. Peale. One game, a big batter hit the ball, but was thrown out on a very close call at first. Mr. Rickey immediately became excited, and he told Dr. Peale, "There's a sermon in that!" Dr. Peale was surprised, and he asked, "What happened? What did I miss?" Mr. Rickey explained, "That big fellow was chewing tobacco. When he hit that ball, he took time to spit, then was out by a whisker. Norman, there's a sermon in that."[221]

Sex

• When film critic Roger Ebert was in the eighth grade at a Catholic school, one of the male students asked a Sister how long one would have to have impure thoughts before the venial sin became a deadly sin. The Sister replied, "There aren't rules for things like that, but I'd say that after five seconds, you're asking for it." Later, the boy and one of his buddies went down into the boy's basement. The boy looked at his father's collection of *Playboy* magazines, while the buddy looked at a stopwatch — every four seconds the buddy hit the boy on the arm.[222]

• In the 1930s, Henry Cadbury, a Quaker, was a New Testament scholar at Harvard. A woman professor shocked many people when she divorced her husband and married someone else. At a faculty party that Mr. Cadbury and his wife, Lydia, attended, the woman professor walked in and Lydia told her husband, quite loudly, "Henry, does thee know that that woman committed adultery?" Mr. Cadbury replied, "I only know, Lydia, that she has not committed it with me."[223]

• St. Augustine resisted becoming a Christian, in part because of the joy of having sexual relations with his mistress of 15 years. He sometimes prayed to God in Latin: *"Da mihi castitatem et continentiam, sed noli modo"* ("Give me chastity and continence, but not yet").[224]

Signs/Inscriptions

• An early boyfriend of comedian Phyllis Diller was Wayne Field Cameron — she even wore an ankle bracelet that had the initials "WFC" engaged on it. However, she didn't want her mother to know about her boyfriend, so when her mother asked what the initials stood for, she answered, "Women's Friendship Circle."[225]

• Louis Agassiz Fuertes was both a painter and a practical joker. Once, he stole a sign with the message "JESUS SAVES," then he placed it in front of a bank.[226]

Ten Commandments

• Valerie Taylor and Sam Silvergilt won prizes for writing essays on "Why I am Proud to be an American" in a contest sponsored by the Daughters of the American Revolution. At the awards banquet, a woman told them, "I don't know if you young people can realize what it means to me to be an American, but I am a collateral descendant of Button Gwinette, who signed the Declaration of Independence." Mr. Silvergilt replied, "Oh, I can understand that — I'm a collateral descendant of the guy who signed the Ten Commandments."[227]

• Famed portrait photographer Yousuf Karsh enjoyed asking his subjects questions as he took their photographs. When he took the photograph of famed humanitarian Albert Schweitzer, he asked him, "Which is the greatest of the Ten Commandments?" Doctor Schweitzer had no problem answering that question. He replied, "Christ gave only one commandment, and that was love."[228]

Travel

• An elderly couple asked Rabbi Marcus Adler of Hanover for advice. They were worried that their son, a traveling salesman, would not remember to recite his daily prayers while he was away from home. The Rabbi replied that the elderly couple should pack their son's handkerchiefs with his *tallith* and *tefillin* (which are used for religious duties such as saying the daily prayers). While the son was away, he wrote home, complaining that he could not find his handkerchiefs. His mother showed the letter to the Rabbi, who advised her to write back, telling him that the Rabbi advised, "Pray to God, and you will find all you seek." The son still did not say his daily prayers, and when he returned home, the Rabbi asked if he had followed the advice in the letter. The young man replied, "Holy Rabbi, how would my praying have anything to do with finding my handkerchiefs. The days of miracles are past." The Rabbi answered, "I still believe that if you would pray in the proper manner you would find what you seek." The young man finally decided to say his daily prayers, and when he opened the bag containing his *tallith* and *tefillin* he found what he was seeking.[229]

• One of the Five Pillars of Islam is making the *hajj* — that is, making a pilgrimage to Mecca. This applies only to those Muslims who are able and can afford to do it, and it need be done only once in a lifetime. Actually, so many Muslims are in the world today that it is physically impossible for them all to make the pilgrimage. Only 2 million Muslims can make the pilgrimage each year due to lack of space in Mecca, and the government of Saudi Arabia uses a quota system for countries, allowing only a certain number of Muslims from each country to make the pilgrimage each year. This actually shows the success of Islam in the modern age. With 1 billion Muslims in the world, and with only 2 million Muslims able to make the pilgrimage each year, for all Muslims alive today to make the pilgrimage would take 500 years.[230]

• The Soviet secret police once interrogated a Russian Jew about a man he had been writing in Israel. The Jew explained that the man he was writing was his brother and not a spy. The secret police told the Jew that it was illegal to correspond with anyone who lived abroad. The Jew thought for a moment and replied, "My brother is at home — I am abroad."[231]

War

• Pastor André Trocmé, the spiritual leader of Le Chambon, a village in southern France that resisted the Nazis and saved the lives of thousands of people, learned about the idea of conscientious objection from a German soldier in World War I. This German soldier worked as a telegrapher during the war, but he refused to carry weapons. Later, during World War II, Pastor André Trocmé did not carry weapons, but nevertheless he was effective in resisting the Nazis and in acting as a role model for others who wished to resist the Nazis.[232]

• An entire platoon of enemy soldiers was captured by a lone Israeli soldier. The Israeli told them, "Don't worry. I'm not going to shoot you. I'm just going to take you to a POW camp." "Thank you," the enemy soldiers said. "You're very kind." "Don't thank me," the Israeli soldier said. "Just be thankful that my husband didn't capture you."[233]

Wisdom

• Bahlool the wise fool was drafted to serve as a soldier although he wished very much for peace. However, when one king decides to go to war against another king, sometimes even a peace-loving person is forced to serve as a soldier in an army. Why? In a war, someone has to fight and die, and kings don't want to fight and die, so they need soldiers to fight and die. An enemy champion challenged any of Bahlool's king's soldiers to step forward for a one-on-one fight to the death. Bahlool's king ordered him to fight the enemy champion, and so Bahlool went out to meet the enemy champion. The enemy champion drew his sword and rushed at Bahlool, who stood still, holding a basket. Because Bahlool did not draw a weapon or run away, but simply stood still, the enemy soldier was puzzled. Bahlool then explained that he had a few questions to ask the enemy champion: "Do you wish to kill me because of a blood feud? Do you wish to kill me because I owe you money that I have not repaid? Have we ever met before? Have you ever heard of me?" The enemy soldier was forced to answer each question with, "No." Bahlool then said, "I have food in my basket. Why don't we have a picnic and see if we can come up with a good reason for you to kill me?" The enemy champion agreed to the picnic, the warring kings saw that Bahlool and the enemy champion were eating together, and for that day at least the two kings called for a truce and no fighting occurred. In addition, Bahlool's king decided that Bahlool was a bad influence on his soldiers and that thereafter Bahlool would be allowed to go home and not be forced to fight in the war.[234]

• What should you do if you have spiritual gifts? A wise man once took a seeker of wisdom with him as he visited a dying man in urgent need of extreme unction. After ministering to the dying man's needs, he noticed a trunk in the death room and asked what was in it. The answer was that the trunk was filled with expensive clothing that the dying man had bought but had never worn, instead allowing them to stay in the trunk where they had rotted with long disuse. After leaving the house, the wise man told the seeker after wisdom, "Remember that trunk filled with rotting clothing. If you have spiritual treasures in your heart, put them into practice now — or they will rot away."[235]

• A parish priest went on a retreat where he met a wise man who was noted for giving questions. The priest went to the wise man and asked for a question. The wise man replied, "What do they need?" The priest was disappointed with the question, but spent a few hours writing out answers to the question. Finally, the priest went back to the wise man and said, "What I really want is a question not about my apostolate, but a question that will help me think about my spiritual life. Can you give me a question like that?" The wise man said, "I understand. The question I give you is this: What do they really need?"[236]

• All too often, money is spent on the military rather than on the people. After Sultan 'Ala'u-'d Din had spent much money fortifying Qonya, he invited Sufi master Baha Veled to view the fortifications. The Sufi master was not impressed, telling the Sultan that the fortifications were a good defense against enemy horsemen, but were no defense at all against the moans of oppressed people. Baha Veled then advised Sultan 'Ala'u-'d Din: "Strive to acquire the blessings of thy subjects. These are a stronghold, compared to which the walls and turrets of the strongest castles are as nothing."[237]

Work

• A Hassid had a problem: the store that he had inherited from his father was not providing a livelihood for him, although it had provided a good livelihood for his father. The Hassid took his problem to the Rebbe, who asked the Hassid what he did when no customers were in the store. The Hassid replied that he read the newspaper. The Rebbe then asked what his father had done when no customers were in the store. The Hassid replied that his father had studied sacred scripture. The Rebbe then explained the Hassid's problem: The Evil One had seen that the Hassid's father was studying sacred scripture and therefore had sent lots of customers to the store to interrupt the study of sacred scripture. The Evil One had later seen the Hassid reading the newspaper and had not bothered to send customers to interrupt the reading of the newspaper.[238]

• An evil man died, and he woke up in a beautiful pleasure palace. A man in white told him, "Devote yourself to pleasure. If you want sex, you can have it. If you want alcohol, you can have it. If you want tobacco, you can have it. If you want food, you can have it. Any pleasure you want, it is yours." For years, the evil man devoted himself to pleasure, and then he said to the man in white, "I have given myself every pleasure I have ever wanted. Now I want something meaningful to do." The man in white said, "I'm very sorry, but that is the only thing that I cannot get for you. Here there is no meaningful work." The evil man complained, "To spend eternity with nothing important to do? I would prefer a thousand times to be in hell!" The man in white replied, "Where do you think you are?"[239]

• Chris Tucker, comedian and actor, started his own foundation originally to help children in South Africa, although the scope of the Chris Tucker Foundation has expanded since then. He once visited Ethiopia, where he talked with two nuns about their work running an orphanage. The two nuns admitted to growing discouraged occasionally. However, one nun had worked with Mother Teresa, and Mother Teresa's words comforted them: "You know how an ocean gets filled up? One drop of rain at a time." The nun identifies the lesson these words teach: "So you just keep doing what you can do."[240]

• The theft of office and other supplies is a major problem for many companies. In the early days of Walt Disney Studios, Bob Beemiller was visited in his studio office at the end of the day by fellow employees John Sibley and Jack Kinney. As Mr. Beemiller prepared to leave, he stuffed his pockets with art and office supplies: animation paper, erasers, pushpins, and pencils. Mr. Sibley asked what he was doing, and Mr. Beemiller explained that he was getting ready to do another job later that day for a friend — a religious film.[241]

• Many Jews consider living in Israel a privilege. The Sheptever Rabbi, Jacob Shimshon, once saw the wife of Rabbi Wolf Zbaraz washing clothing in a washtub. She told him, "This linen is not mine. I am washing it for others, and I am being paid for the task. But I feel no regrets. No sacrifice is too great for the privilege of living in Eretz Yisrael."[242]

• The Hasidic masters treated workers and work with respect. The founder of Hasidism, the Baal Shem Tov, told a story about a man who made stockings. Before making the stockings, the man prayed, and while making the stockings, the man recited psalms that he knew by heart.[243]

• At a small-town parish in Uvalde, Texas, a very serious four-year-old asked Msgr. Vincent Fecher, "Are you Jesus?" He replied, "No, but I work for him."[244]

Yom Kippur

• Rabbi Israel Salanter (1810-1883) began serving as the Rabbi of Kovno in 1848. When a cholera epidemic broke out, he turned the synagogue into a hospital, saying, "God would much prefer that his house be used for the suffering and the poor than just a place where the rich can worship." The cholera epidemic continued. On the eve of Yom Kippur, Rabbi Salanter asked a physician what the people needed to survive the epidemic. The physician replied that if the people had rest and food, they would survive. This presented a problem because Yom Kippur is a day of fasting. On Yom Kippur, Rabbi Salanter appeared before the people and explained that although fasting is normally observed on Yom Kippur, in light of the epidemic, breaking the fast would not be a sin. The people started to protest, but the good Rabbi quieted their protest by eating a piece of bread.[245]

• On the eve of Yom Kippur, the Baal Shem Tov walked joyfully down the street, shocking a bystander. After all, the bystander reminded the Baal Shem Tov, Yom Kippur is the Day of Judgment, when God judges each person either positively or negatively. If God were to give the Baal Shem Tov a negative verdict, that was nothing to be happy about. And if the Baal Shem Tov was certain that God would give him a positive verdict, wouldn't his sureness show conceit? The Baal Shem Tov replied, "The verdict is entirely irrelevant to my joy. I am rejoicing because there is both a Judge and judgment in the World."[246]

Zen

• Zen masters always stick up for the little people and sometimes bring down the high and mighty a little. The Zen master of Tofuku once was visited by a VIP who sent him a card that said, "Kitagaki, the governor of Kyoto, has just arrived and requests to meet with you." The Zen master of Tofuku sent back the message, "I don't want to meet with Kitagaki, the governor of Kyoto." Kitagaki may have been a VIP, but he was not stupid, and he realized what was wrong. He took back his card, crossed out a few words, and sent it again to the Zen master. This time, the note said, "Kitagaki has just arrived and requests to meet with you." This time, the Zen master sent back the message, "Welcome."[247]

• Daniel Pinkwater is known for his humorous books for children, and one of his inspirations is Zen master Ho Chi, a statue of whom Mr. Pinkwater keeps on his desk. Ho Chi dropped out of the rat race to wander around with a bag of cookies in his hands. Children liked him because he would give them cookies, and adults were perturbed because Ho Chi was not chasing the cheese the way they were doing. Adults would ask him to do what they were doing and chase the cheese. Ho Chi always replied to these meddlesome adults, "Give me a penny." Mr. Pinkwater says about Ho Chi, "He's like me."[248]

• A thief once entered the hut of Zen master Ryokan, only to find there was nothing to steal. However, Ryokan, who was outside, saw the thief and said to him, "You have come a long way to visit, and you should not return empty-handed. Please take my clothes as a gift." After the thief had taken his clothes, Ryokan sat naked in the moonlight, looking at the moon, and said, "Poor fellow, I wish I could give him this moon."[249]

• A large part of Zen Buddhism is living in the present moment rather than living in the past or the future. A new monk asked Zen master Joshu, "What is the first principle of Zen?" Joshu asked the new monk, "Have you eaten your supper?" The new monk answered, "Yes." Joshu then told the new monk, "Now wash your bowl."[250]

Appendix A: Bibliography

Adams, Joey. *The God Bit*. Boston, MA: G.K. Hall & Co., 1975.

Adler, David A. *A Hero and the Holocaust: The Story of Janusz Korczak and His Children*. New York: Holiday House, 2002.

Adler, David A. *We Remember the Holocaust*. New York: Henry Holt and Company, 1989.

Aflaki, Shams al-Din Ahmad. *Legends of the Sufis: Selected Anecdotes from the Work Entitled, The Acts of the Adepts by Shemsu-'D-Din Ahmed, El Eflaki*. London: Theosophical Publishing House, 1976.

Al-Amily, Hussain M., compiler. *The Book of Arabian Wisdom: Proverbs and Anecdotes*. Oxford: New Internationalist Publications, Ltd., 2003.

Ali, Hana. *More Than a Hero: Muhammad Ali's Life Lessons Presented Through His Daughter's Eyes*. New York: Pocket Books, 2000.

Alley, Ken. *Awkward Christian Soldiers*. Wheaton, IL: Harold Shaw Publishers, 1998.

Altman, Linda Jacobs. *Slavery and Abolition in American History*. Berkeley Heights, NJ: Enslow Publications, Inc., 1999.

Axelrod, Toby. *In the Camps: Teens Who Survived the Nazi Concentration Camps*. New York: The Rosen Publishing Group, Inc., 1999.

Banker, Stan. *Walk Cheerfully the Middleroad*. Richmond, IN: Friends United Press, 1994.

Blue, Lionel, and Jonathan Magonet. *The Jewish Guide to the Here and the Hereafter*. New York: Crossroad Publishing Company, 1989.

Boxer, Tim. *The Jewish Celebrity Hall of Fame*. New York: Shapolsky Publishers, 1987.

Brown, Joe E. *Laughter is a Wonderful Thing*. As told to Ralph Hancock. New York: A.S. Barnes and Co., 1956.

Brown, Michèle and Ann O'Connor. *Hammer and Tongues: A Dictionary of Women's Wit and Humour*. London: J.M. Dent and Sons, Ltd., 1986.

Buber, Martin. *The Way of Man: According to the Teaching of Hasidism*. New York: The Citadel Press, 1966.

Byars, Ann. *Oskar Schindler: Saving Jews from the Holocaust*. Berkeley Heights, NJ: Enslow Publishers, Inc., 2005.

Camp, Carole Ann. *American Astronomers*. Springfield, NJ: Enslow Publications, Inc., 1996.

Certner, Simon, editor. *101 Jewish Stories for Schools, Clubs and Camps*. New York: Jewish Education Committee Press, 1961.

Charles, Helen White, collector and editor. *Quaker Chuckles and Other True Stories About Friends*. Oxford, OH: H.W. Charles, 1961.

Clark, Charles. *Islam*. San Diego, CA: Lucent Books, Inc., 2002.

Clercq, Tanaquil Le. *The Ballet Cook Book*. New York: Stein and Day, Publishers, 1966.

Cleary, Thomas, translator. *Zen Antics: A Hundred Stories of Enlightenment*

Clower, Jerry. *Ain't God Good!* Waco, TX: Word Books, Publisher, 1975.

Coelho, Paulo. *Confessions of a Pilgrim*. Interviews by Juan Arias. Translated by Anne McLean. London: HarperCollinsPublishers, 2001.

Cox, Clinton. *Mark Twain: America's Humorist, Dreamer, Prophet*. New York: Scholastic, Inc., 1995.

Dharma Realm Buddhist University, Buddhist Text Translation Society, adaptors and translators. *Human Roots: Buddhist Stories for Young Readers*. Talmadge, CA: Buddhist Text Translation Society, 1982.

Deedy, John. *A Book of Catholic Anecdotes*. Allen, TX: Thomas More, 1997.

Diebold, Reinhard, collector and editor. *The Book of Good Deeds: 1914-1918*. Translated by Hellmut and Letitia Lehmann-Haupt. New York: Farrar & Rinehart, 1933.

Diller, Phyllis. *Like a Lampshade in a Whorehouse: My Life in Comedy*. With Richard Buskin. London: Penguin Group, 2005.

Dosick, Rabbi Wayne. *The Business Bible: Ten Commandments for Creating an Ethical Workplace*. New York: William Morrow and Company, Inc., 1993.

Draper, Allison Stark. *Pastor André Trocmé: Spiritual Leader of the French Village Le Chambon*. New York: The Rosen Publishing Group, Inc., 2001.

Epstein, Lawrence J. *A Treasury of Jewish Anecdotes*. Northvale, NJ: Jason Aronson, Inc., 1989.

Epstein, Lawrence J. *A Treasury of Jewish Inspirational Stories*. Northvale, NJ: Jason Aronson, Inc., 1993.

Erskine, Carl. *Carl Erskine's Tales from the Dodger Dugout*. Champaigne, IL: Sports Publishing, Inc., 2000.

Fadiman, James and Robert Frager. *Essential Sufism*. San Francisco, CA: HarperSanFrancisco, 1997.

Fager, Chuck. *Quakers are Funny! A New Collection of Quaker Humor*. Falls Church, VA: Kimo Press, 1987.

Farzan, Massud. *Another Way of Laughter: A Collection of Sufi Humor*. New York: E.P. Dutton & Co., Inc., 1973.

Fecher, Msgr. Vincent. *"The Lord and I": Vignettes from the Life of a Parish Priest*. New York: Alba House, 1990.

Fesquet, Henri, collector. *Wit and Wisdom of Good Pope John*. Translated by Salvator Attanasio. New York: P.J. Kenedy & Sons, 1964.

Franks, A.H., editor. *Pavlova: A Collection of Memoirs*. New York: Da Capo Press, Inc., 1956.

Fremon, David K. *The Holocaust Heroes*. Springfield, NJ: Enslow Publications, Inc., 1998.

Fuller, Gerald. *Stories for All Seasons*. Mystic, CT: Twenty-Third Publications, 1996.

Garagiola, Joe. *It's Anybody's Ballgame*. New York: Jove Books, 1988.

Gaster, Moses. *The Exempla of the Rabbis: Being a Collection of Exempla, Apologues and Tales Culled from Hebrew Manuscripts and Rare Hebrew Books*. New York: Ktav Publishing House, Inc., 1968.

Gelberman, Rabbi Joseph H. *Zen Judaism: Teaching Tales of a Kabbalistic Rabbi*. With Lesley Sussman. Freedom, CA: The Crossing Press, 2001.

Gershick, Zsa Zsa. *Gay Old Girls*. Los Angeles, CA: Alyson Books, 1998.

Gignoux, Jane Hughes. *Some Folk Say: Stories of Life, Death, and Beyond*. New York: FoulkeTale Publishing, 1998.

Glatzer, Nahum N., editor. *Hammer on the Rock: A Short Midrash Reader*. Translated by Jacob Sloan. New York: Schocken Books, 1962.

Glavich, Mary Kathleen, S.N.D. *Catholic School Kids Say the Funniest Things*. New York: Paulist Press, 2002.

Glenn, Menahem G. *Israel Salanter: Religious-Ethical Thinker*. New York: Bloch Publishing Company, 1953.

Goble, Paul. *Hau Kola* Hello Friend. Katonah, NY: Richard C. Owens Publishers, Inc., 1994.

Goldin, Barbara Diamond. *A Child's Book of the Midrash: 52 Jewish Stories from the Sages*. Northvale, NJ: Jason Aronson Inc., 1990.

Goldin, Barbara Diamond, reteller. *Creating Angels: Stories of* Tzedakah. Northvale, NJ: Jason Aronson, Inc., 1996.

Goldwasser, Rabbi Dovid. *It Happened in Heaven: Personal Stories of Inspiration*. Jerusalem: Feldheim Publishers, 1995.

González-Balado, José Luis, compiler. *Mother Teresa: In My Own Words*. New York: Gramercy Books, 1996.

Goodman, Philip. *Rejoice in Thy Festival*. New York: Bloch Publishing Company, 1956.

Greenberg, Keith Elliot. *An Armenian Family*. Minneapolis, MN: Lerner Publications Company, 1997.

Hacohen, Rabbi Shmuel Avidor, compiler. *Touching Heaven, Touching Earth: Hassidic Humor and Wit*. Tel Aviv: Sadan Publishing, 1976.

Halamandaris, Val, editor and compiler. *Faces of Caring*. Washington, D.C.: Caring Publishing, 1992.

Henry, Lewis C. *Humorous Anecdotes About Famous People*. Garden City, NY: Halcyon House, 1948.

Himelstein, Shmuel. *A Touch of Wisdom, A Touch of Wit*. Brooklyn, NY: Mesorah Publications, Limited, 1991.

Himelstein, Shmuel. *Words of Wisdom, Words of Wit*. Brooklyn, NY: Mesorah Publications, Ltd., 1993.

Hindman, Jane F. *An Ordinary Saint: The Life of John Neumann*. New York: Arena Lettres, 1977.

Holland, Merlin. *The Wilde Album*. New York: Henry Holt and Company, 1997.

Holloway, Gary. *Saints, Demons, and Asses: Southern Preacher Anecdotes*. Bloomington, IN: Indiana University Press, 1989.

Hyman, Dick. *Potomac Wind and Wisdom: Jokes, Lies, and True Stories By and About America's Politics and Politicians*. Brattleboro, VT: The Stephen Greene Press, 1980.

Irving, Gordon, compiler. *The Wit of the Scots*. London: Leslie Frewin Publishers, Inc., 1969.

Isaacs, Ronald H., and Kerry M. Olitzky. *Sacred Moments: Tales from the Jewish Life Cycle*. Northvale, NJ: Jason Aronson, Inc., 1995.

Jacobs, J. Vernon, compiler. *450 True Stories from Church History*. Grand Rapids, MI: Wm. B. Eerdmans Publishing Company, 1955.

Karsh, Yousuf. *Karsh: A Sixty-Year Retrospective*. Boston, MA: Little, Brown and Company, 1996.

Kennedy, Robert E. *Zen Spirit, Christian Spirit: The Place of Zen in Christian Life*. New York: Continuum Publishing Company, 1995.

Kertzer, Morris N. *Tell Me, Rabbi*. New York: Bloch Publishing Company, 1976.

Kinney, Jack. *Walt Disney and Other Assorted Characters: An Unauthorized Account of the Early Years at Disney's*. New York: Harmony Books, 1988.

Kornfield, Jack, and Christina Feldman. *Soul Food: Stories to Nourish the Spirit and the Heart*. San Francisco, CA: HarperSanFrancisco, 1996. This is a revised edition of their 1991 book *Stories of the Spirit, Stories of the Heart*.

Kovacs, Deborah, and James Preller. *Meet the Authors and Illustrators: Volume Two*. New York: Scholastic, Inc., 1993.

Kuhn, Betsy. *Angels of Mercy: The Army Nurses of World War II*. New York: Atheneum Books for Young Readers, 1999.

Kustanowitz, Esther. *The Hidden Children of the Holocaust: Teens Who Hid from the Nazis*. New York: The Rosen Publishing Group, Inc., 1999.

Leonard, Sheldon. *And the Show Goes On: Broadway and Hollywood Adventures.* New York: Limelight, 1994.

Linkletter, Art. *I Didn't Do It Alone: The Autobiography of Art Linkletter.* As told to George Bishop. Ottawa, IL: Caroline House Publishers, Inc., 1980.

Linkletter, Art. *I Wish I'd Said That! My Favorite Ad-Libs of All Time.* Garden City, NY: Doubleday & Co., Inc., 1968.

Maccoby, Hyam, chooser and translator. *The Day God Laughed: Sayings, Fables and Entertainments of the Jewish Sages.* With conversations between Wolf Mankowitz and Hyam Maccoby. New York: St. Martin's Press, 1978.

Marston, Elsa. *Muhammad of Mecca: Prophet of Islam.* New York: Franklin Watts, 2001.

Maser, Frederick E., and Robert Drew Simpson. *If Saddlebags Could Talk: Methodist Stories and Anecdotes.* Franklin, TN: Providence House Publishers, 1998.

Meltzer, Milton. *Rescue: The Story of How Gentiles Saved Jews in the Holocaust.* New York: Harper and Row, Publishers, 1988.

Mendelsohn, S. Felix. *Let Laughter Ring.* Philadelphia, PA: The Jewish Publication Society of America, 1941.

Millman, Isaac. *Hidden Child.* New York: Farrar, Straus and Giroux, 2005.

Mindess, Harvey. *The Chosen People? A Testament, Both Old and New, to the Therapeutic Power of Jewish Wit and Humor.* Los Angeles, CA: Nash Publishing Corporation, 1972.

Molen, Sam. *Take 2 and Hit to Right.* Philadelphia, PA: Dorrance and Company, 1959.

Mullen, Tom. *Laughing Out Loud and Other Religious Experiences.* Waco, TX: Word Books, 1983.

Mullen, Tom. *Living Longer and Other Sobering Possibilities.* Richmond, IN: Friends United Press, 1996.

Neches, Solomon Michael. *Humorous Tales of Latter Day Rabbis.* New York: George Dobsevage, 1938.

Netzach, editor. *Chesed: The World is Built upon Kindness.* Edited and published by Netzach, a project of Mercaz HaTorah of California. North Hollywood, CA: Netzach, 1985.

Netzley, Patricia D. *Buddhism.* San Diego, CA: Lucent Books, Inc., 2002.

Neuwirth, Allan. *They'll Never Put That on the Air: An Oral History of Taboo-Breaking TV Comedy.* New York: Allworth Press, 2006.

Orgill, Roxanne. *Mahalia: A Life in Gospel Music.* Cambridge, MA: Candlewick Press, 2002.

Parker, John F. *"If Elected, I Promise ...."* Garden City, NY: Doubleday & Co., Inc., 1960.

Pellowski, Michael J. *Baseball's Funniest People*. New York: Sterling Publishing Co., 1997.

Petuchowski, Jakob J., translator and editor. *Our Masters Taught: Rabbinic Stories and Sayings*. New York: Crossroad, 1982.

Phares, Ross. *Bible in Pocket, Gun in Hand: The Story of Frontier Religion*. Garden City, NY: Doubleday & Company, Inc., 1964.

Phayer, Michael, and Eva Fleischner. *Cries in the Night: Women Who Challenged the Holocaust*. Kansas City, MO: Sheed and Ward, 1997. Jessica Scheetz also helped write this book.

Pochocki, Ethel. *One-of-a-Kind Friends: Saints and Heroes for Kids*. Cincinnati, OH: St. Anthony Messenger Press, 1994.

Podgórecki, Adam. *The Stories of Si-Tien*. London: Poets' and Painters' Press, 1971.

Podgórecki, Adam. *The Tales of Si-tien*. London: Poets' and Painters' Press, 1973.

Porter, Alyene. *Papa was a Preacher*. New York: Abingdon Press, 1944.

Rabinowicz, Rabbi Dr. H. *A Guide to Hassidism*. New York: Thomas Yoseloff, 1960.

Reidelbach, Maria. *Completely MAD: A History of the Comic Book and Magazine*. Boston, MA: Little, Brown and Company, 1991.

Reps, Paul, compiler. *Zen Flesh, Zen Bones*. Rutland, VT: Charles E. Tuttle Co., 1957.

Richardson, Ann, and Dietmar Bolle, editors. *Wise Before Their Time: People with AIDS and HIV Talk About Their Lives*. London: Fount, 1992.

Rolph, Daniel N. *My Brother's Keeper: Union and Confederate Soldiers' Acts of Mercy during the Civil War*. Mechanicsburg, PA: Stackpole Books, 2002.

Rowell, Edward K., editor. *Humor for Preaching and Teaching*. Grand Rapids, MI: Baker Books, 1996.

Salkin, Jeffrey K. *Being God's Partner: How to Find the Hidden Link Between Spirituality and Your Work*. Woodstock, VT: Jewish Lights Publishing, 1994.

Samra, Cal and Rose, editors. *Holy Hilarity*. Colorado Springs, CO: WaterBrook Press, 1999.

Samra, Cal and Rose, editors. *Holy Humor*. Colorado Springs, CO: WaterBrook Press, 1997.

Schuman, Michael A. *Elie Wiesel: Voice from the Holocaust*. Hillside, NJ: Enslow Publishers, Inc., 1994.

Sessions, William H., collector. *Laughter in Quaker Grey*. York, England: William Sessions, Limited, 1966.

Shuker, Nancy. *Maya Angelou: America's Poetic Voice*. Woodbridge, CT: Blackbirch Press, 2001.

Silver, Eric. *The Book of the Just: The Unsung Heroes Who Rescued Jews from Hitler*. New York: Grove Press, 1992.

Silverman, William B. *Rabbinic Wisdom and Jewish Values*. New York: Union of American Hebrew Congregations, 1971.

Smith, Elson. *The Blooper Man: The Rip Sewell Story*. Bellevue, PA: J. Pohl Associates, 1981.

Smith, H. Allen. *The Compleat Practical Joker*. Garden City, NY: Doubleday and Company, Inc., 1953.

Smith, H. Allen. *People Named Smith*. Garden City, NY: Doubleday & Company, Inc., 1950.

Spalding, Henry D. *Jewish Laffs*. Middle Village, NY: Jonathan David Publishers, Inc., 1982.

Spencer, John. *Workers for Humanity*. London: George G. Harrap and Co., Ltd., 1962.

Stevens, William Oliver. *Famous Humanitarians*. New York: Dodd, Mead & Company, 1953.

Streissguth, Thomas. *Hinduism*. San Diego, CA: Lucent Books, 2002.

Strug, Kerri. *Landing on My Feet: A Diary of Dreams*. With John P. Lopez. Kansas City, MO: Andrews McMeel Publishing, 1997.

Tanner, Stephen. *Opera Antics and Anecdotes*. Toronto, Canada: Sound and Vision, 1999.

Taylor, Glenhall. *Before Television: The Radio Years*. New York: A.S. Barnes and Company, 1979.

Telushkin, Rabbi Joseph. *Jewish Wisdom: Ethical, Spiritual, and Historical Lessons from the Great Works and Thinkers*. New York: William Morrow and Company, Inc., 1994.

Thompson, Joe. *Growing Up with "Shoeless Joe."* Greenville, SC: Burgess International, 1997.

Tsai, Chih-Chung (editor and illustrator) and Kok Kok Kiang (translator). *The Book of Zen*. Singapore: Asiapac, 1990.

Udall, Morris K. *Too Funny to be President*. With Bob Neuman and Randy Udall. New York: Henry Holt and Company, 1988.

Van Dyke, Dick. *Faith, Hope and Hilarity*. Edited by Ray Parker. Garden City, NY: Doubleday and Company, Inc., 1970.

Wagenknecht, Edward. *Merely Players*. Norman, OK: University of Oklahoma Press, 1966.

Ward, Hiley H., editor. *Ecumania: The Humor That Happens When Catholics, Jews, and Protestants Come Together*. New York: Association Press, 1968.

Zen Buddhism: An Introduction to Zen with Stories, Parables, and Zoan Riddles Told by the Zen Masters. Mount Vernon, NY: Peter Pauper Press, 1959.

Appendix B: About the Author

It was a dark and stormy night. Suddenly a cry rang out, and on a hot summer night in 1954, Josephine, wife of Carl Bruce, gave birth to a boy — me. Unfortunately, this young married couple allowed Reuben Saturday, Josephine's brother, to name their first-born. Reuben, aka "The Joker," decided that Bruce was a nice name, so he decided to name me Bruce Bruce. I have gone by my middle name — David — ever since.

Being named Bruce David Bruce hasn't been all bad. Bank tellers remember me very quickly, so I don't often have to show an ID. It can be fun in charades, also. When I was a counselor as a teenager at Camp Echoing Hills in Warsaw, Ohio, a fellow counselor gave the signs for "sounds like" and "two words," then she pointed to a bruise on her leg twice. Bruise Bruise? Oh yeah, Bruce Bruce is the answer!

Uncle Reuben, by the way, gave me a haircut when I was in kindergarten. He cut my hair short and shaved a small bald spot on the back of my head. My mother wouldn't let me go to school until the bald spot grew out again.

Of all my brothers and sisters (six in all), I am the only transplant to Athens, Ohio. I was born in Newark, Ohio, and have lived all around Southeastern Ohio. However, I moved to Athens to go to Ohio University and have never left.

At Ohio U, I never could make up my mind whether to major in English or Philosophy, so I got a bachelor's degree with a double major in both areas, then I added a master's degree in English and a master's degree in Philosophy. Currently, and for a long time to come, I publish a weekly humorous column titled "Wise Up!" for *The Athens News* and I am an English instructor at Ohio U.

If all goes well, I will publish one or two books a year for the rest of my life. (On the other hand, a good way to make God laugh is to tell Her your plans.)

By the way, my sister Brenda Kennedy writes romances such as *A New Beginning* and *Shattered Dreams*.

Appendix C: Some Books by David Bruce

Anecdote Collections

250 Anecdotes About Opera
250 Anecdotes About Religion
250 Anecdotes About Religion: Volume 2
250 Music Anecdotes
Be a Work of Art: 250 Anecdotes and Stories
The Coolest People in Art: 250 Anecdotes
The Coolest People in the Arts: 250 Anecdotes
The Coolest People in Books: 250 Anecdotes
The Coolest People in Comedy: 250 Anecdotes
Create, Then Take a Break: 250 Anecdotes
Don't Fear the Reaper: 250 Anecdotes
The Funniest People in Art: 250 Anecdotes
The Funniest People in Books: 250 Anecdotes
The Funniest People in Books, Volume 2: 250 Anecdotes
The Funniest People in Books, Volume 3: 250 Anecdotes
The Funniest People in Comedy: 250 Anecdotes
The Funniest People in Dance: 250 Anecdotes
The Funniest People in Families: 250 Anecdotes
The Funniest People in Families, Volume 2: 250 Anecdotes
The Funniest People in Families, Volume 3: 250 Anecdotes
The Funniest People in Families, Volume 4: 250 Anecdotes
The Funniest People in Families, Volume 5: 250 Anecdotes
The Funniest People in Families, Volume 6: 250 Anecdotes
The Funniest People in Movies: 250 Anecdotes
The Funniest People in Music: 250 Anecdotes
The Funniest People in Music, Volume 2: 250 Anecdotes
The Funniest People in Music, Volume 3: 250 Anecdotes
The Funniest People in Neighborhoods: 250 Anecdotes
The Funniest People in Relationships: 250 Anecdotes
The Funniest People in Sports: 250 Anecdotes
The Funniest People in Sports, Volume 2: 250 Anecdotes
The Funniest People in Television and Radio: 250 Anecdotes
The Funniest People in Theater: 250 Anecdotes

The Funniest People Who Live Life: 250 Anecdotes
The Funniest People Who Live Life, Volume 2: 250 Anecdotes
The Kindest People Who Do Good Deeds, Volume 1: 250 Anecdotes
The Kindest People Who Do Good Deeds, Volume 2: 250 Anecdotes
Maximum Cool: 250 Anecdotes
The Most Interesting People in Movies: 250 Anecdotes
The Most Interesting People in Politics and History: 250 Anecdotes
The Most Interesting People in Politics and History, Volume 2: 250 Anecdotes
The Most Interesting People in Politics and History, Volume 3: 250 Anecdotes
The Most Interesting People in Religion: 250 Anecdotes
The Most Interesting People in Sports: 250 Anecdotes
The Most Interesting People Who Live Life: 250 Anecdotes
The Most Interesting People Who Live Life, Volume 2: 250 Anecdotes
Reality is Fabulous: 250 Anecdotes and Stories
Resist Psychic Death: 250 Anecdotes
Seize the Day: 250 Anecdotes and Stories

[1]Source: Elsa Marston, *Muhammad of Mecca: Prophet of Islam*, p. 50.

[2] Source: Patricia D. Netzley, *Buddhism*, p. 44.

[3]Source: Massud Farzan, *Another Way of Laughter*, p. 9.

[4] Source: Tom Danehy, "Read along as Tom reveals his wants and needs." *Tucson Weekly*. 10 January 2008 <http://www.tucsonweekly.com/gbase/Opinion/Content?oid=oid:105185>.

[5]Source: Tim Boxer, *The Jewish Celebrity Hall of Fame*, p. 78.

[6]Source: Tim Boxer, *The Jewish Celebrity Hall of Fame*, p. 176.

[7]Source: Joe Garagiola, *It's Anybody's Ballgame*, pp. 93-94.

[8]Source: Michael J. Pellowski, *Baseball's Funniest People*, p. 51.

[9]Source: Stan Banker, *Walk Cheerfully the Middleroad*, p. 101.

[10]Source: Ken Alley, *Awkward Christian Soldiers*, p. 89.

[11] Source: Maria Reidelbach, *Completely MAD*, pp. 191-192.

[12]Source: Rabbi Joseph H. Gelberman, *Zen Judaism: Teaching Tales of a Kabbalistic Rabbi*, p. 27. The pages of this volume are unnumbered, but I started counting with the Introduction as page 1.

[13]Source: Rabbi Joseph Telushkin, *Jewish Humor*, pp. 151-152.

[14]Source: Netzach, editor, *Chesed: The World is Built upon Kindness*, p. 30.

[15] Source: Val Halamandaris, editor and compiler, *Faces of Caring*, pp. 30-31.

[16] Source: Michele Hanson, "Those who don't care will never cough up for charity — so what's the point of sending free Biros and slippers?" *The Guardian*. 2 January 2007 <http://www.guardian.co.uk/g2/story/0,,1981084,00.html>.

[17] Source: Barbara Diamond Goldin, reteller, *Creating Angels: Stories of Tzedakah*, pp. 125-126.

[18]Source: Rabbi Joseph Telushkin, *Jewish Wisdom*, p. 23.

[19]Source: Barbara Diamond Goldin, *A Child's Book of the Midrash: 52 Jewish Stories from the Sages*, pp. 9-12.

[20] Source: Thomas Streissguth, *Hinduism*, pp. 56-57.

[21]Source: Mary Kathleen Glavich, S.N.D., *Catholic School Kids Say the Funniest Things*, p. 19.

[22]Source: Moses Gaster, *The Exempla of the Rabbis*, p. 65.

[23]Source: José Luis González-Balado, compiler, *Mother Teresa: In My Own Words*, p. 20.

[24] Source: Eric Silver, *The Book of the Just: The Unsung Heroes Who Rescued Jews from Hitler*, pp. 22-31.

[25] Source: Betsy Kuhn, *Angels of Mercy: The Army Nurses of World War II*, p. 31.

[26] Source: Emily Wilson, "The Commercialization of Christmas: What Would Jesus Buy?" 23 November 2007 <http://www.alternet.org/mediaculture/68485/>.

[27]Source: Alyene Porter, *Papa was a Preacher*, pp. 147-148.

[28] Source: Edward Rothstein, "Celebrating Abraham Joshua Heschel, one of America's best-known Jewish figures." *International Herald-Tribune*. 27 December 2007 <http://www.iht.com/articles/2007/12/27/arts/24conn.php>.

[29]Source: Daniel N. Rolph, *My Brother's Keeper*, p. 84.

[30] Source: Isaac Millman, *Hidden Child*, pp. 49-50.

[31] Source: Yousuf Karsh, *Karsh: A Sixty-Year Retrospective*, p. 141.

[32]Source: A.H. Franks, editor, *Pavlova: A Collection of Memoirs*, pp. 88-89.

[33]Source: Hiley H. Ward, editor, *Ecumania*, p. 44.

[34] Source: Stephen Tanner, *Opera Antics and Anecdotes*, p. 26.

[35] Source: Deborah Kovacs and James Preller, *Meet the Authors and Illustrators: Volume Two*, p. 45.

[36]Source: Kerri Strug, *Landing on My Feet*, p. 60.

[37]Source: Maureen Lipman, "Ireland: land of charm, humour, breathtaking vistas ... and delicious homemade mayonnaise?" *The Guardian*. 21 August 2006 <http://www.guardian.co.uk/g2/story/0,,1854627,00.html>.

[38]Source: Tom Mullen, *Living Longer and Other Sobering Possibilities*, p. 68.

[39]Source: Dick Van Dyke, *Faith, Hope, and Hilarity*, p. 69.

[40]Source: Edward Wagenknecht, *Merely Players*, p. 191.

[41]Source: Joe Thompson, *Growing Up with "Shoeless Joe,"* p. 123.

[42]Source: Helen White Charles, collector and editor, *Quaker Chuckles*, p. 3.

[43] Source: Carl Erskine, *Carl Erskine's Tales from the Dodger Dugout*, p. 90.

[44]Source: Cal and Rose Samra, editors, *More Holy Humor*, p. 40.

[45] Source: Tanaquil Le Clercq, *The Ballet Cook Book*, p. 396.

[46] Source: Jane Hughes Gignoux, *Some Folk Say: Stories of Life, Death, and Beyond*, pp. 52-54.

[47] Source: Ronald H. Isaacs and Kerry M. Olitzky, *Sacred Moments: Tales from the Jewish Life Cycle*, pp. 190-191.

[48] Source: Ann Richardson and Dietmar Bolle, editors, *Wise Before Their Time: People with AIDS and HIV Talk About Their Lives*, pp. 36-40.

[49] Source: Michael A. Schuman, *Elie Wiesel: Voice from the Holocaust*, pp. 112, 114.

[50] Source: José Luis González-Balado, compiler, *Mother Teresa: In My Own Words*, p. 69.

[51] Source: Lawrence J. Epstein, *A Treasury of Jewish Inspirational Stories*, pp. 158-159.

[52] Source: Hana Ali, *More Than a Hero*, p. 40.

[53] Source: Jane Hughes Gignoux, *Some Folk Say: Stories of Life, Death, and Beyond*, pp.142-143/

[54] Source: Cal and Rose Samra, *Holy Hilarity*, pp. 83-84.

[55] Source: Louise Chipley Slavicek, *Confucianism*, pp. 25, 27.

[56] Source: Merlin Holland, *The Wilde Album*, pp. 24-25. The envelope appears in a plate following p. 16.

[57] Source: Ethel Pochocki, *One-of-a-Kind Friends*, p. 46.

[58] Source: Cal and Rose Samra, *Holy Humor*, p. 120.

[59] Source: Gordon Irving, compiler, *The Wit of the Scots*, p. 38.

[60] Source: Cal and Rose Samra, *Holy Hilarity*, pp. 118-120.

[61] Source: John Deedy, *A Book of Catholic Anecdotes*, p. 243.

[62] Source: Jane F. Hindman, *An Ordinary Saint: The Life of John Neumann*, pp. 87-88.

[63] Source: "Interview by Michael Kress: The 'Super-Believer.'" June 2007 <http://www.beliefnet.com/story/188/story_18880_1.html>.

[64] Source: Paul Goble, *Hau Kola* Hello Friend, pp. 7, 14, 17, 23, 27, 30.

[65] Source: Shmuel Himelstein, *Words of Wisdom, Words of Wit*, p. 94.

[66] Source: Wayne Dosick, *The Business Bible*, pp. 43-44.

[67] Source: Louise Chipley Slavicek, *Confucianism*, pp. 25, 80.

[68] Source: Paulo Coelho, *Confessions of a Pilgrim*, pp. 94-95.

[69]Source: Robert E. Kennedy, *Zen Spirit, Christian Spirit*, p. 75.

[70]Source: Thomas Cleary, translator, *Zen Antics*, pp. 17-18.

[71]Source: Carole Ann Camp, *American Astronomers*, p. 73-75.

[72]Source: James Fadiman and Robert Frager, *Essential Sufism*, p. 136.

[73]Source: Paul Reps, *Zen Flesh, Zen Bones*, pp. 71-72.

[74]Source: Mary Kathleen Glavich, S.N.D., *Catholic School Kids Say the Funniest Things*, p. 29.

[75]Source: Shmuel Himelstein, *A Touch of Wisdom, A Touch of Wit*, p. 30.

[76] Source: Penelope H. Bevan, "Let children be children." 3 June 2007 <http://www.sfgate.com/cgi-bin/article.cgi?file=/chronicle/archive/2007/06/03/INGE5Q5QCO1.DTL>.

[77]Source: Adam Podgórecki, *The Stories of Si-Tien*, p. 28.

[78]Source: Adam Podgórecki, *The Tales of Si-tien*, p. 39.

[79]Source: Adam Podgórecki, *The Stories of Si-Tien*, pp. 33-34.

[80] Source: Frederick E. Maser and Robert Drew Simpson, *If Saddlebags Could Talk*, p. 10

[81]Source: Carole Ann Camp, *American Astronomers*, p. 71.

[82] Source: John Spencer, *Workers for Humanity*, p. 77.

[83]Source: Menahem G. Glenn, *Israel Salanter: Religious-Ethical Thinker*, pp. 86-87.

[84]Source: Rabbi Dr. H. Rabinowicz, *A Guide to Hassidism*, p. 24.

[85] Source: Rabbi Shmuel Avidor Hacohen, compiler, *Touching Heaven, Touching Earth: Hassidic Humor and Wit*, p. 86.

[86]Source: Simon Certner, editor, *101 Jewish Stories for Schools, Clubs and Camps*, p. 136.

[87]Source: Moses Gaster, *The Exempla of the Rabbis*, p. 55.

[88]Source: Adam Podgórecki, *The Tales of Si-tien*, p. 35.

[89] Source: Thomas Streissguth, *Hinduism*, p. 61.

[90]Source: Gerald Fuller, *Stories for All Seasons*, p. 25.

[91]Source: José Luis González-Balado, compiler, *Mother Teresa: In My Own Words*, p. 93.

[92] Source: "Interview by Dena Ross: George Foreman's Second Chance." July 2007 <http://www.beliefnet.com/story/219/story_21994_1.html>.

[93] Source: Joe E. Brown, *Laughter is a Wonderful Thing*, pp. 116-117.

[94] Source: Roxanne Orgill, *Mahalia: A Life in Gospel Music*, pp. 38-39.

[95] Source: Esther Kustanowitz, *The Hidden Children of the Holocaust*, pp. 42, 45, 52.

[96] Source: Rabbi Shmuley Boteach, "Sparring With the Almighty." 4 June 2006 <http://www.beliefnet.com/story/192/story_19236_1.html>.

[97] Source: Ralph Sanders, "You Can't Say We Don't Know How to Bake." 9 November 2006 <http://www.andrewtobias.com/newcolumns/061109.html>.

[98] Source: Ross Phares, *Bible in Pocket, Gun in Hand*, p. 48.

[99] Source: Ethel Pochocki, *One-of-a-Kind Friends*, pp. 50-51.

[100] Source: Rabbi Joseph H. Gelberman, *Zen Judaism: Teaching Tales of a Kabbalistic Rabbi*, p. 57. The pages of this volume are unnumbered, but I started counting with the Introduction as page 1.

[101] Source: Gary Holloway, *Saints, Demons, and Asses*, pp. 91-92.

[102] Source: Joey Adams, *The God Bit*, p. 73.

[103] Source: Simon Certner, editor, *101 Jewish Stories for Schools, Clubs and Camps*, p. 53.

[104] Source: Martin Buber, *The Way of Man*, pp. 9-10.

[105] Source: Lionel Blue and Jonathan Magonet, *The Jewish Guide to the Here and the Hereafter*, p. 181.

[106] Source: J. Vernon Jacobs, compiler, *450 True Stories from Church History*, p. 120.

[107] Source: Martin Buber, *The Way of Man*, pp. 40-41.

[108] Source: Michèle Brown and Ann O'Connor, *Hammer and Tongues*, p. 106.

[109] Source: Barbara Diamond Goldin, reteller, *Creating Angels: Stories of Tzedakah*, pp. 47-49.

[110] Source: Ann Byars, *Oskar Schindler: Saving Jews from the Holocaust*, pp. 13, 36, 127-128.

[111] Source: Reinhard Diebold, collector and editor, *The Book of Good Deeds: 1914-1918*, pp. 171-172.

[112] Source: Eric Silver, *The Book of the Just: The Unsung Heroes Who Rescued Jews from Hitler*, pp. 1, 123-125.

[113] Source: Michael Phayer and Eva Fleischner, *Cries in the Night: Women Who Challenged the Holocaust*, pp. 1-3, 12-13.

[114] Source: David K. Fremon, *The Holocaust Heroes*, p. 61.

[115] Source: William Oliver Stevens, *Famous Humanitarians*, pp. 98-99.

[116] Source: Milton Meltzer, *Rescue: The Story of How Gentiles Saved Jews in the Holocaust*, p. 19.

[117] Source: Betsy Kuhn, *Angels of Mercy: The Army Nurses of World War II*, pp. 42-43, 51.

[118] Source: Hana Ali, *More Than a Hero*, pp. 44-45.

[119] Source: David A. Adler, *We Remember the Holocaust*, p. 93.

[120] Source: Netzach, editor, *Chesed: The World is Built upon Kindness*, pp. 17-18.

[121] Source: Isaac Millman, *Hidden Child*, p. 15.

[122] Source: Daniel N. Rolph, *My Brother's Keeper*, p. 1.

[123] Source: Tsai Chih Chung (editor and illustrator) and Kok Kok Kiang (translator), *The Book of Zen*, p. 113.

[124] Source: Elsa Marston, *Muhammad of Mecca: Prophet of Islam*, p. 91.

[125] Source: David A. Adler, *A Hero and the Holocaust: The Story of Janusz Korczak and His Children*. The pages of this children's book are unnumbered.

[126] Source: Michael Phayer and Eva Fleischner, *Cries in the Night: Women Who Challenged the Holocaust*, pp. 95-99, 103, 142-143.

[127] Source: Milton Meltzer, *Rescue: The Story of How Gentiles Saved Jews in the Holocaust*, p. 33.

[128] Source: David A. Adler, *We Remember the Holocaust*, pp. 101-102.

[129] Source: Ann Byars, *Oskar Schindler: Saving Jews from the Holocaust*, pp. 116-117, 129.

[130] Source: Toby Axelrod, *In the Camps: Teens Who Survived the Nazi Concentration Camps*, pp. 22-24.

[131] Source: Lionel Blue and Jonathan Magonet, *The Jewish Guide to the Here and the Hereafter*, p. 93.

[132] Source: David K. Fremon, *The Holocaust Heroes*, p. 74.

[133] Source: Hyam Maccoby, chooser and translator, *The Day God Laughed: Sayings, Fables and Entertainments of the Jewish Sages*, pp. 61-63.

[134]Source: Lewis C. Henry, *Humorous Anecdotes About Famous People*, p. 131.

[135]Source: Nahum N. Glatzer, editor, *Hammer on the Rock*, p. 20.

[136] Source: Ann Richardson and Dietmar Bolle, editors, *Wise Before Their Time: People with AIDS and HIV Talk About Their Lives*, p. 115.

[137]Source: Jack Kinney, *Walt Disney and Other Assorted Characters*, pp. 132-133.

[138] Source: Maria Reidelbach, *Completely MAD*, p. 9.

[139]Source: Cal and Rose Samra, *Holy Hilarity*, p. 152.

[140]Source: Wayne Dosick, *The Business Bible*, pp. 65-66.

[141]Source: José Luis González-Balado, compiler, *Mother Teresa: In My Own Words*, p. 49.

[142]Source: Allan Neuwirth, *They'll Never Put That on the Air*, p. 142.

[143] Source: Nancy Shuker, *Maya Angelou: America's Poetic Voice*, p. 89.

[144]Source: Jakob J. Petuchowski, translator and editor, *Our Masters Taught*, pp. 89-90.

[145] Source: Catherine O'Sullivan, "Married? Then do not read this column." *Tucson Weekly*. 12 June 2008 <http://www.tucsonweekly.com/gbase/Opinion/Content?oid=oid:111886>.

[146]Source: Art Linkletter, *I Didn't Do It Alone*, p. 122.

[147]Source: Jack Kornfield and Christina Feldman, *Soul Food*, pp. 43-44.

[148]Source: Cal and Rose Samra, *Holy Hilarity*, p. 152.

[149]Source: Henry D. Spalding, *Jewish Laffs*, p. 37.

[150] Source: Hyam Maccoby, chooser and translator, *The Day God Laughed: Sayings, Fables and Entertainments of the Jewish Sages*, pp. 141-142.

[151] Source: Joe Bob Briggs, aka John Bloom, "Review of *Jesus and Archaeology*, edited by James H. Charlesworth." 15 December 2007 <http://www.joebobbriggs.com/bookclub/reviews/jesusandarcheology.asp>.

[152] Source: Hussain M. Al-Amily, compiler, *The Book of Arabian Wisdom*, p. 127.

[153] Source: Paulo Coelho, *Confessions of a Pilgrim*, p. 204.

[154] Source: John Spencer, *Workers for Humanity*, pp. 35-36, 38-39.

[155] Source: Alyene Porter, *Papa was a Preacher*, p. 15.

[156] Source: James Fadiman and Robert Frager, *Essential Sufism*, pp. 27-28, 82-83.

[157] Source: William B. Silverman, *Rabbinic Wisdom and Jewish Values*, p. 204.

[158] Source: *Zen Buddhism: An Introduction to Zen with Stories, Parables, and Zoan Riddles Told by the Zen Masters*, p. 56.

[159] Source: Reinhard Diebold, collector and editor, *The Book of Good Deeds: 1914-1918*, pp. 153-154.

[160] Source: Morris K. Udall, *Too Funny to be President*, pp. 243-244.

[161] Source: Val Halamandaris, editor and compiler, *Faces of Caring*, pp. 20-21.

[162] Source: Michèle Brown and Ann O'Connor, *Hammer and Tongues*, p. 38.

[163] Source: Elson Smith, *The Blooper Man*, pp. 19-20.

[164] Source: Philip Goodman, *Rejoice in Thy Festival*, pp. 164-165.

[165] Source: Lawrence J. Epstein, *A Treasury of Jewish Anecdotes*, pp. 167-168.

[166] Source: Edward K. Rowell, editor, *Humor for Preaching and Teaching*, p. 75.

[167] Source: Mary Blye Howe, "Preparing for the High Holy Days." http://www.beliefnet.com/story/175/story_17563_1.html. September 2005.

[168] Source: Roxanne Orgill, *Mahalia: A Life in Gospel Music*, pp. 26-27.

[169] Source: Amy Ruth, *Mother Teresa*, pp. 29, 80.

[170] Source: H. Allen Smith, *People Named Smith*, p. 59.

[171] Source: Henri Fesquet, collector, *Wit and Wisdom of Good Pope John*, p. 140.

[172] Source: Ronald H. Isaacs and Kerry M. Olitzky, *Sacred Moments: Tales from the Jewish Life Cycle*, p. 235.

[173] Source: Lawrence J. Epstein, *A Treasury of Jewish Anecdotes*, p. 70.

[174] Source: S. Felix Mendelsohn, *Let Laughter Ring*, pp. 56-57.

[175] Source: Morris K. Udall, *Too Funny to be President*, p. 10.

[176] Source: Art Linkletter, *I Wish I'd Said That!*, p. 95.

[177] Source: Linda Jacob Altman, *Slavery and Abolition in American History*, pp. 5-7.

[178] Source: Charles Clark, *Islam*, p. 19.

[179] Source: Lisa Kaiser, "'It's the Most Liberating Thing': Six Milwaukeeans tell their coming-out stories." The *Shepherd Express*. 7 June 2007 <http://shepherd-express.com/

1editorialbody.lasso?-token.folder=2007-06-07&-token.story=177343.113121&-token.sub|

[180] Source: Clinton Cox, *Mark Twain: America's Humorist, Dreamer, Prophet*, pp. 12-13.

[181] Source: H. Allen Smith, *The Compleat Practical Joker*, p. 110.

[182] Source: Jerry Clower, *Ain't God Good!*, p. 63.

[183] Source: Michael A. Schuman, *Elie Wiesel: Voice from the Holocaust*, p. 91.

[184] Source: Sam Molen, *Take 2 and Hit to Right*, p. 121.

[185] Source: Tom Mullen, *Laughing Out Loud and Other Religious Experiences*, p. 46.

[186] Source: Dick Hyman, *Potomac Wind and Wisdom*, p. 49.

[187] Source: Tom Mullen, *Living Longer and Other Sobering Possibilities*, p. 8.

[188] Source: Rabbi Dovid Goldwasser, *It Happened in Heaven*, p. 159.

[189] Source: Joey Adams, *The God Bit*, p. 72.

[190] Source: Jerry Clower, *Ain't God Good!*, p. 168.

[191] Source: Allan Neuwirth, *They'll Never Put That on the Air*, pp. 190-193.

[192] Source: Tom Mullen, *Laughing Out Loud and Other Religious Experiences*, p. 27.

[193] Source: S. Felix Mendelsohn, *Let Laughter Ring*, p. 29.

[194] Source: Glenhall Taylor, *Before Television*, pp, 96-97.

[195] Source: Morris K. Udall, *Too Funny to be President*, p. 196.

[196] Source: Dharma Realm Buddhist University, Buddhist Text Translation Society, adaptors and translators, *Human Roots: Buddhist Stories for Young Readers*, pp. 1-4. I have freely adapted this story.

[197] Source: Barbara Diamond Goldin, *A Child's Book of the Midrash: 52 Jewish Stories from the Sages*, pp. 71-72.

[198] Source: Solomon Michael Neches, *Humorous Tales of Latter Day Rabbis*, pp. 86-87.

[199] Source: Joe Garagiola, *It's Anybody's Ballgame*, pp. 81-82.

[200] Source: Purple Gene, "Purple Gene Reviews 'How to Cook Your Life[1].'" BartCop Entertainment. 25 October 2007 <http://suprmchaos.com/bcEnt-Thu-102507.index.html>.

[201] Source: Helen White Charles, collector and editor, *Quaker Chuckles*, p. 46.

[202] Source: Jane F. Hindman, *An Ordinary Saint: The Life of John Neumann*, p. 102.

[203] Source: Phyllis Diller, *Like a Lampshade in a Whorehouse: My Life in Comedy*, p. 37.

[204] Source: Sam Molen, *Take 2 and Hit to Right*, pp. 77-78.

[205] Source: Keith Elliot Greenberg, *An Armenian Family*, p. 25.

[206] Source: Shmuel Himelstein, *A Touch of Wisdom, A Touch of Wit*, p. 123.

[207] Source: Thomas Cleary, translator, *Zen Antics*, p. 69.

[208] Source: William Oliver Stevens, *Famous Humanitarians*, p. 114.

[209] Source: Morris N. Kertzer, *Tell Me, Rabbi*, p. 100.

[210] Source: Linda Jacob Altman, *Slavery and Abolition in American History*, pp. 53-54.

[211] Source: Allison Stark Draper, *Pastor André Trocmé: Spiritual Leader of the French Village Le Chambon*, pp. 5, 9-12.

[212] Source: Esther Kustanowitz, *The Hidden Children of the Holocaust*, pp. 24-25, 48.

[213] Source: Morris N. Kertzer, *Tell Me, Rabbi*, pp. 166-167.

[214] Source: Philip Goodman, *Rejoice in Thy Festival*, pp. 36-37.

[215] Source: Lawrence J. Epstein, *A Treasury of Jewish Anecdotes*, p. 114.

[216] Source: Dan Wakefield: "St. Dorothy: Why Dorothy Day should be canonized. September 2006 <http://www.beliefnet.com/story/23/story_2379_1.html>.

[217] Source: Shams al-Din Ahmad Aflaki, *Legends of the Sufis*, pp. 97-98.

[218] Source: Chuck Fager, *Quakers are Funny!*, pp. 36-37.

[219] Source: Patricia D. Netzley, *Buddhism*, p. 24.

[220] Source: Frederick E. Maser and Robert Drew Simpson, *If Saddlebags Could Talk*, p. 50.

---

1.   http://imdb.com/title/tt0943512/

[221] Source: Carl Erskine, *Carl Erskine's Tales from the Dodger Dugout*, pp. 29-30.

[222] Source: Roger Ebert, "Superbad." 16 August 2007 <http://rogerebert.suntimes.com/apps/pbcs.dll/article?AID=/20070816/REVIEWS/70817001>.

[223] Source: Chuck Fager, *Quakers are Funny!*, p. 98.

[224] Source: John Deedy, *A Book of Catholic Anecdotes*, p. 15.

[225] Source: Phyllis Diller, *Like a Lampshade in a Whorehouse: My Life in Comedy*, p. 40.

[226] Source: H. Allen Smith, *The Compleat Practical Joker*, p. 136.

[227] Source: Zsa Zsa Gershick, *Gay Old Girls*, pp. 173-174.

[228] Source: Yousuf Karsh, *Karsh: A Sixty-Year Retrospective*, p. 144.

[229] Source: Solomon Michael Neches, *Humorous Tales of Latter Day Rabbis*, pp. 66-67.

[230] Source: Charles Clark, *Islam*, pp. 32-33.

[231] Source: Lawrence J. Epstein, *A Treasury of Jewish Inspirational Stories*, p. 190.

[232] Source: Allison Stark Draper, *Pastor André Trocmé: Spiritual Leader of the French Village Le Chambon.*, p. 17.

[233] Source: Harvey Mindess, *The Chosen People?*, pp. 94-95.

[234] Source: Hussain M. Al-Amily, compiler, *The Book of Arabian Wisdom*, p. 186.

[235] Source: Paulo Coelho, "Human stains" *The Guardian*. 20 April 2007 <http://books.guardian.co.uk/extracts/story/0,,2062052,00.html>.

[236] Source: Jack Kornfield and Christina Feldman, *Soul Food*, pp. 124-125.

[237] Source: Shams al-Din Ahmad Aflaki, *Legends of the Sufis*, p. 7.

[238] Source: Rabbi Shmuel Avidor Hacohen, compiler, *Touching Heaven, Touching Earth: Hassidic Humor and Wit*, p. 62.

[239] Source: Paulo Coelho, "Human stains" *The Guardian*. 20 April 2007 <http://books.guardian.co.uk/extracts/story/0,,2062052,00.html>.

[240] Source: Terry Lawson, "Chris Tucker's African awakening." 9 August 2007 <http://www.popmatters.com/pm/news/article/47039/chris-tuckers-african-awakening/>.

[241] Source: Jack Kinney, *Walt Disney and Other Assorted Characters*, p. 127.

[242]Source: Rabbi Dr. H. Rabinowicz, *A Guide to Hassidism*, pp. 129-130.

[243]Source: Jeffrey K. Salkin, *Being God's Partner*, p. 68.

[244]Source: Msgr. Vincent Fecher, *"The Lord and I": Vignettes from the Life of a Parish Priest*, p. 11.

[245]Source: Lawrence J. Epstein, *A Treasury of Jewish Anecdotes*, pp. 199-200.

[246]Source: Shmuel Himelstein, *Words of Wisdom, Words of Wit*, p. 43.

[247] Source: Paulo Coelho, "Human stains" *The Guardian*. 20 April 2007 <http://books.guardian.co.uk/extracts/story/0,,2062052,00.html>.

[248] Source: Deborah Kovacs and James Preller, *Meet the Authors and Illustrators: Volume Two*, p. 125.

[249]Source: Paul Reps, *Zen Flesh, Zen Bones*, p. 27.

[250] Source: *Zen Buddhism: An Introduction to Zen with Stories, Parables, and Zoan Riddles Told by the Zen Masters*, p. 33.